The Wealth Mindset Reset

The Wealth Mindset Reset

Reprogram Your Beliefs for Financial Success

Rami de Vries

Mindful Pages

Published in 2025

ISBN: 9789371343251 (PB)
ISBN: 9789371344258 (eBook)

Published by

Mindful Pages
Imprint of Alpha Editions LLC
312 W. 2nd St #1834
Casper, WY 82601, USA

This book was developed using advanced writing tools to support the drafting and ideation process. All content has been thoughtfully curated, refined, and reviewed to ensure quality and relevance.

Content

Introduction
The Invisible Wallet

We don't merely spend money—we enact belief systems. Every financial act, whether it's swiping a card at the checkout, deciding on a profession, negotiating pay, or forgoing a holiday you've long dreamed of, arises from a tapestry of underlying convictions. These convictions, often hidden from view, reflect deep narratives around worthiness, safety, success, and what's possible. They don't emerge by chance. Rather, they are passed down, absorbed through culture, etched in emotional memory, and quietly reinforced every time we glance at a receipt or click "buy now." While mainstream discussions around financial hardship tend to fixate on surface-level metrics—too little income, too many expenses, not enough saving—the truth operates at a subtler, more psychological level. Behind every budget lies a biography. And within each biography, a belief system at work.

The prevailing money discourse is outward-facing: earn more, spend less, invest wisely, buy property, rinse, repeat. These practicalities have their place, to be sure. But they're not where real change begins. Many people, with the best of intentions, take advice, sign up for workshops, or try out the latest budgeting software, only to circle back to the same place—discouraged, stuck, or strangely self-defeating. Why does this happen? Because they're addressing symptoms, not causes. The true terrain of transformation is internal. Until we bring our financial conditioning into conscious awareness—what this book refers to as our *inner economy*—any progress is precarious, vulnerable to the next stressor, or emotional spike.

Here's where the journey starts—with a somewhat unconventional, yet vital premise: your financial outcomes are shaped not merely by what you do, but by what you believe. Imagine you're carrying an "invisible wallet." Not one made of leather or pixels, but of convictions. It's always with you. It determines not just how you spend, but what you feel entitled to, what you feel guilty wanting, and even what you subconsciously repel. Unlike your banking app, this wallet doesn't ping you with alerts or neatly reconcile itself. It runs in the background, scripting your financial life. This isn't about assigning blame—it's about illuminating what's been unconscious. You cannot alter what remains hidden. But once brought to light, belief patterns can be rewritten.

So, we begin with the internal economy—that nuanced and often neglected world of emotions, memories, ideas, and assumptions that influence every financial move. Just as countries operate with complex economic policies and inherited debts, individuals do too. The initial chapters will invite you to explore your early financial environment: the words spoken about money, the tensions you absorbed, the permissions or prohibitions you encountered, the sense of scarcity or abundance that surrounded you. These aren't minor moments. They're structural. From them arise your subconscious "scripts"—often rooted in fear, guilt, lack, or burden—that shape how you engage with money as an adult.

But early life is just one layer. This book also considers the cultural and societal voices that condition our relationship with money. Advertisements, Instagram influencers, fairy tales, political narratives—all of them carry implicit messages about wealth: who deserves it, how it's earned, what it symbolises. These myths are rarely challenged directly, yet they infiltrate our psyche. They can sow doubt, erode agency, and reinforce roles we never consciously chose. If you've ever felt uneasy about wanting more, ashamed of earning too little, or stuck in resentment about your finances, know that these feelings are not purely personal. They often trace back to stories we've absorbed rather than realities we've authored.

That is why this book does not pretend to be a step-by-step manual on money management. Instead, it invites you to undertake something far more radical: to rewire the operating system that governs your relationship with money. Before we delve into practices—like budgeting or investing—we will lay a new psychological groundwork. One grounded not in fear or scarcity, but in insight, self-trust, and sovereignty.

The chapters are deliberately sequenced to reflect this unfolding. Chapter One guides you in mapping your inner financial landscape. You'll revisit early experiences, decode inherited beliefs, and begin tracing how these moments shaped your patterns. It's an archaeological dig, of sorts—uncovering the emotional and symbolic roots of your financial identity.

Chapter Two brings focus to that identity. How do you show up in relationship to money? Are you the compulsive saver, the reluctant earner, the guilt-ridden giver, the hoarder, the minimalist? These archetypes aren't quirks. They're expressions of deeper emotional themes—deservingness, control, belonging, safety. Here, you'll begin reshaping this identity consciously, rooted in who you are becoming, not who you've been conditioned to be.

With Chapter Three, the attention turns to belief itself. How do beliefs form? How do they hide? And how can they be dismantled and rebuilt? Drawing from psychology and neuroscience, this chapter equips you to spot limiting beliefs—those quiet scripts that say "I'll never get ahead" or "Money corrupts"—and replace them not with naïve positivity, but with truth-backed alternatives. It's about creating a belief ecosystem that supports your evolving financial reality.

Then we delve into emotion, often the invisible hand behind our financial decisions. Chapter Four explores the emotional circuitry of money—compulsive spending, guilt-laden saving, financial anxiety. These aren't moral failings; they're nervous system responses. You'll learn to spot your "money trauma" behaviours, whether that means overspending under stress, freezing in indecision, or bending financially to avoid conflict. Techniques from somatic psychology and emotional intelligence will support your shift from reactivity to intentionality.

In Chapter Five, language becomes the lens. The phrases we use—"I can't afford that," "I'm terrible with money"—are not just statements. They're affirmations, constantly reaffirming our financial stance. This chapter helps you shift your money vocabulary—without veering into denial or toxic optimism—so that it reflects possibility, responsibility, and choice. You'll even craft your own "wealth scripts," tailored narratives that articulate your evolving story with clarity and agency.

Next, in Chapter Six, we begin translating internal work into outward habits. The goal here is sustainability, not self-discipline via guilt. Think of practical systems—automated savings, behavioural triggers, rituals that reinforce your values. The idea isn't to build a perfect system, but one that gently holds your new mindset. Change sticks best when it's aligned with identity, not forced through pressure.

Chapter Seven then opens the door to a more expansive question: what does wealth mean to you? Not in abstract terms, but as a lived vision. Forget hustle culture. Forget performative wealth. This chapter helps you shape a definition of prosperity that aligns with your values and includes joy, rest, contribution, and beauty. It's especially crucial for those whose gifts—whether in healing, teaching, art, or care—have been undervalued in the economic narrative. You deserve to thrive, not just survive.

Finally, Chapter Eight zooms out. Here, we move from stabilising your finances to envisioning what's next. You'll be encouraged to dream bigger, to step beyond survival thinking and embrace growth. This chapter offers guidance on navigating risk, cultivating supportive environments, and trusting the cyclical nature of wealth creation. Crucially, you'll see how mindset and income exist in a feedback loop—shifting one inevitably alters the other.

Through it all, the core message remains: you are not broken. Your financial struggles are not character flaws. You've been running a programme—largely invisible, often inherited. But programming can be changed. Patterns can be rewritten. This isn't just about getting your money "in order." It's about transforming how you relate to it, from the inside out.

The Wealth Mindset Reset is not meant to be skimmed or conquered. It's a companion, a guide to return to, to sit with. Each chapter offers both insight and practice. Because money, whether we like it or not, is one of our most enduring relationships. It is worthy of care, of reflection, of courage.

By the time you reach the end, you won't simply "know more" about money. You will have begun to inhabit a different way of being with it—one rooted in clarity, sovereignty, and a quiet sense of enough. And from that foundation, real wealth—not just in currency, but in meaning—can begin to grow.

Chapter 1
The Money You Can't See

When we picture money, we tend to see the measurable parts—the digits on a screen, the monthly payslip, the stack of unopened bank letters, perhaps the ups and downs of an investment account. These are the figures we tally, the indicators we're taught to monitor. Yet they're only half the story. Hidden beneath the surface lies a subtler, more influential force: our internal economy. This one can't be charted on a spreadsheet. It doesn't operate with pounds and pence, but with convictions, emotions, and inherited scripts. And make no mistake—it's this quiet architecture that truly governs our financial lives.

Like a country with its own economic policy, history, and unspoken rules, every individual harbours a personal economy. If we were to coin a phrase—call it your psychological GDP: Generated Default Programming. It's the subconscious engine that decides whether you lowball your worth, stash money compulsively, dread investing, or squirm at the thought of charging what you're actually worth. These tendencies rarely stem from logic. They're driven instead by emotion, past experience, and deeply embedded narratives. And so, to speak meaningfully about money—beyond tactics and trendlines—we must begin here.

So much of this internal blueprint is laid down early. Childhood, after all, isn't just where we learn language or ride a bike—it's where we first absorb the emotional frequency of money. Was it spoken of freely or with tension? Was it bound to security, or control? Generosity, or guilt? A child who witnesses quiet dread whenever a bill lands on the doormat may grow up equating money with danger. Another, repeatedly hearing "we can't afford it" without context, might internalise the message that desire itself is somehow shameful. These messages, even when subtly expressed, embed themselves with startling persistence.

Take Tara, for instance—a thriving entrepreneur, outwardly confident and successful. And yet, she routinely undercharged clients and over-delivered to the point of burnout. A pattern that made no financial sense. Upon reflection, she recognised echoes from her upbringing: parents who, though kind and hardworking, lived by a creed of self-sacrifice. Comfort, to them, bordered on indulgence; money, while necessary, was never to be trusted. Tara, despite her accomplishments, had unknowingly inherited a moral discomfort with financial ease. Her adult decisions were being steered by a child's emotional inheritance.

And this is the heart of it: you cannot out-earn your beliefs. Not sustainably. Which is why the first step toward financial transformation isn't budgeting or investing—it's unearthing. Begin by mapping out key money memories. Not just what happened, but what was felt. Was receiving a gift accompanied by guilt? Did thrift earn you praise? Was debt spoken of with dread, or not at all? This isn't a forensic audit. It's a gentle reckoning. You're not seeking culprits—you're tracing origins.

Closely entwined with early impressions is the notion of financial trauma. It might sound dramatic at first glance, but its psychological grounding is solid. Trauma, in essence, is what happens when an experience overwhelms our capacity to process. And money—especially when entangled with survival—can do exactly that. Think sudden job loss, eviction, persistent financial instability, or the grinding weight of inherited poverty. These aren't just tough times. They leave an imprint—neurological, emotional, behavioural.

Consider James. Raised in a household where eviction loomed like weather, he now earns more than enough. And yet, he checks his bank balance obsessively, sometimes a dozen times a day. Rationally, he knows he's secure. But his body doesn't. His nervous system remains primed for collapse. Financial planning alone won't soothe that alarm. What he needs isn't just strategy—it's repair. Somatic grounding. Emotional integration. A rewriting of the belief that money equals instability.

This is the dimension often overlooked in traditional finance education. It presumes a rational actor. But humans, under pressure, are anything but. We hoard, we binge, we deny, we defer. Healing, then, is not sentimental—it's structural. Until we offer grace to the parts of us that act out under financial stress, we're merely managing symptoms, not root causes.

And it's not only our upbringing that carves these patterns. We live in a world saturated with stories about money—broadcast through films, adverts, schoolyard myths, and the glossy haze of Instagram. "Money is power," we're told, which sounds bold until it calcifies into the belief that seeking wealth makes you domineering. Or the old chestnut: "the rich are greedy." A comforting narrative, perhaps, if you've never felt comfortable with abundance. These beliefs, often unspoken, form the cultural fog in which we all move.

The media doesn't help. Wealthy characters are cast as emotionally barren or ethically compromised. Meanwhile, poverty is romanticised—linked with purity, struggle, or artistic authenticity. Social media, for its part, offers a continuous feed of curated lifestyles, rarely disclosing what lies beneath: debt, burnout, the quiet despair of performative affluence. We begin to assess ourselves not by what we value, but by what we perceive others are achieving.

The antidote? Conscious editing. Ask yourself: what financial narratives am I absorbing? Whose definition of success have I borrowed without examination? And more pointedly—do these ideas serve me? This isn't simply about becoming media-savvy. It's about reclaiming the lens through which we view value, wealth, and self-worth.

To anchor this work, try imagining your financial life as a story. What's its title? What genre—drama, farce, epic quest? Who are its central characters? What turning points shaped the plot? First job, first debt, a moment of windfall or betrayal? This exercise may feel abstract, even indulgent. But it's not. It's one of the most effective ways to turn money from a source of anxiety into a source of narrative coherence. Because once you see the story, you're no longer just living it—you can begin to edit it.

Ultimately, what this exploration makes painfully, beautifully clear is that money has never been just about transactions. It is about security. About identity. About memory and belonging and risk and reward. It is about the countless small, often unspoken choices we make—not from spreadsheets, but from the beliefs we hold about who we are and what we deserve.

This chapter, then, doesn't offer tidy answers or prescriptive steps. It asks a deeper question: are you willing to see? To really see the forces that shape your financial choices, long before you sit down with a calculator or open an investment account? If so, then what follows can be more than educational. It can be transformative.

Awareness, after all, is not passive. It's catalytic. And when you start to observe the invisible economy you've been operating within—consciously or not—you gain something more valuable than any financial windfall. You gain the ability to choose. To rewrite. To begin again. And that, in the truest sense, is wealth.

The Internal Economy

Every nation has an economy—a system of exchange, a flow of resources, a framework of incentives and disincentives that determine prosperity or struggle. Economists measure these systems through gross domestic product (GDP), inflation rates, employment figures, and consumer confidence. Yet what is far less acknowledged is that individuals, too, operate within their own personal economic systems. Each of us carries an internal economy—an intricate psychological framework composed of beliefs, emotions, memories, and narratives—that silently governs our financial decisions. It does not issue currency or appear on tax returns, but its influence is arguably more powerful than any market fluctuation or fiscal policy. It is, quite literally, your personal GDP: *Generated Default Programming.*

This internal economy is rarely examined, yet it is constantly active. It shapes how you feel when you check your bank balance. It informs your reaction to a financial windfall or an unexpected expense. It whispers in moments of ambition and shouts during episodes of self-doubt. Despite its subtlety, it forms the foundation of your financial life. To understand it is not merely to gain insight—it is to reclaim control.

At its core, the internal economy is built upon belief systems. These beliefs, often inherited rather than consciously chosen, act as filters through which we interpret financial experiences. Some are overt, such as "money doesn't grow on trees," while others operate more subtly: a discomfort with asking for a raise, a habitual underpricing of your services, or a persistent sense of guilt when spending on yourself. These patterns do not emerge randomly; they are reflections of internal scripts developed over years of observation, emotion, and repetition.

Consider the case of Ana, a talented graphic designer who consistently underquoted her services. Despite glowing feedback from clients and increasing demand, she found herself hesitant to raise her prices. When prompted to explore her beliefs around money, Ana recalled a childhood where financial modesty was prized. Her parents, both social workers, spoke of wealth with scepticism and subtly equated financial ambition with greed. Without ever being directly instructed, Ana absorbed the belief that to desire more was to betray her values. This internalised narrative capped her income, not because of market conditions or a lack of skill, but because of a subconscious allegiance to familial values.

Our emotions further entrench these belief systems. Neuroscience has shown that financial decisions are heavily influenced by the limbic system—the brain's emotional centre—rather than the rational prefrontal cortex. This explains why people often make financial choices that defy logic: spending impulsively when anxious, avoiding bills due to shame, or hoarding savings out of fear despite long-term goals to invest. Emotions act as both fuel and friction in our internal economies. They determine the speed and direction of our financial behaviour, often without conscious recognition.

Take, for instance, the behavioural finance concept of *loss aversion.* Studies by Kahneman and Tversky revealed that the psychological pain of losing money is roughly twice as powerful as the pleasure of gaining it. This emotional bias leads individuals to make conservative choices that may hinder long-term wealth creation—such as holding onto underperforming investments or avoiding entrepreneurial risks. These are not merely strategic errors. They are emotional reflexes embedded in the internal economy's operating system.

Adding another layer to this complexity is the narrative structure of the human mind. We do not simply remember facts about our financial past; we construct stories. These stories help us make sense of experiences, but they also cement our identity. A person who has struggled with debt may develop a narrative of being "bad with money," and this identity can become self-fulfilling. Even when circumstances change, the internal script remains. Attempts at financial improvement may then feel foreign or unsustainable, because they conflict with the established narrative.

This dynamic is illustrated by the story of Marcus, who after years of financial struggle landed a well-paying job in tech. Despite the increase in income, Marcus found himself living paycheque to paycheque. He justified his spending as "finally living," but underneath was a deeper issue: his self-concept had not caught up with his new reality. He still identified as someone who barely scraped by. As a result, he unconsciously found ways to recreate the emotional atmosphere of scarcity—overspending, neglecting savings, and avoiding long-term planning. His behaviour was not a lack of discipline, but a symptom of narrative incongruence.

Understanding your internal economy, then, requires a multifaceted approach—one that blends introspection with psychological insight. Start by noticing your financial patterns without judgement. What behaviours feel automatic? What situations trigger anxiety, avoidance, or overcompensation? Often, the most revealing data points are not financial statements, but emotional ones. When you look at your financial decisions through the lens of curiosity rather than critique, you begin to map the contours of your inner economic system.

From there, reflection becomes a powerful diagnostic tool. Recall your first encounters with money. Were they infused with freedom or restriction, stability or chaos? Did your caregivers model financial confidence or fear? How was wealth discussed in your household—was it admired, envied, condemned, or simply ignored? These early imprints form the foundational settings of your internal economy. They become the emotional language with which you relate to earning, spending, saving, and giving.

It is also vital to examine the cultural and societal overlays on your personal economy. We are constantly immersed in ideological messaging about what money signifies. From advertising to politics, from religious traditions to workplace dynamics, we absorb countless narratives: that success equals income, that wealth corrupts, that hard work is morally superior to passive income. These messages do not just influence our opinions; they shape our thresholds of what feels normal, desirable, or attainable. Left unchallenged, they calcify into unconscious ceilings.

A telling example can be found in the concept of the "upper limit problem," a term coined by psychologist Gay Hendricks. It refers to the tendency for individuals to self-sabotage when life surpasses their internalised threshold for success or happiness. In financial terms, this might manifest as suddenly incurring large expenses after receiving a bonus, or feeling inexplicably anxious after achieving a long-awaited income goal. The internal economy, rooted in old narratives, resists change—even positive change—if it threatens the emotional equilibrium we unconsciously associate with safety.

Fortunately, internal economies, like national ones, are not fixed. They can be audited, restructured, and renewed. But unlike changing careers or opening a new savings account, this kind of transformation begins at the cognitive-emotional level. It involves identifying the underlying beliefs driving your decisions, questioning their validity, and consciously choosing more aligned alternatives. Neuroplasticity research has demonstrated the brain's remarkable ability to rewire itself through repetition and emotional salience. What this means practically is that financial transformation is possible not through willpower alone, but through the deliberate cultivation of new beliefs reinforced by meaningful action.

For instance, someone who believes "I'm terrible with money" might start by noticing how often they repeat this phrase—internally or aloud. By substituting it with a gentler, more constructive statement like "I'm learning to understand my finances," and pairing that with manageable, confidence-building actions such as reviewing their accounts weekly, they begin to shift their internal economic identity. Over time, this creates a new feedback loop: positive action reinforces a new belief, which in turn inspires more empowered behaviour.

Yet this work is not linear. Internal economies are influenced by past wounds, current pressures, and future anxieties. Like any complex system, they require ongoing attention and adaptability. However, the rewards of this internal audit are profound. By aligning your psychological patterns with your financial goals, you reduce inner conflict, increase decision-making clarity, and open the door to sustained prosperity—not just in income, but in your relationship with money as a whole.

Understanding and reshaping your internal economy is not simply a precursor to wealth-building. It is the essence of it. Financial freedom is not defined by external numbers alone. It is defined by internal coherence—the alignment of what you believe, feel, and do. When your beliefs support your goals, when your emotions reinforce your decisions, and when your narratives expand your possibilities rather than constrict them, you begin to operate not from default, but from design.

This chapter invites you to become the chief economist of your own life. To audit your beliefs, regulate your emotional flows, and rewrite the narratives that govern your financial world. The tools and strategies that follow in this book will equip you to build external wealth. But they can only take root if the internal economy has been prepared. When your inner world supports your outer goals, money ceases to be a source of confusion or anxiety—it becomes an instrument of alignment, intention, and true abundance.

Financial Echoes from Childhood

Long before we ever earn our first paycheque or open a bank account, we inherit a relationship with money. It is not taught in any formal classroom, nor outlined in explicit rules. Rather, it is absorbed—quietly, emotionally, and often unconsciously—through the routines, tensions, silences, and spoken or unspoken values of our childhood homes. These early financial experiences function much like emotional DNA. They become the templates through which we interpret, respond to, and often unconsciously replicate financial behaviour in adulthood. What may appear as a budgeting issue or poor impulse control often traces back to patterned responses forged in early life.

Childhood is a potent period of psychological formation, and money is one of the most emotionally charged subjects we encounter, even if it is rarely discussed directly. Children are extraordinarily sensitive to the emotional currents that surround adult conversations. A slammed door after a conversation about bills, an anxious glance when asked for pocket money, or a celebration over a promotion—these events, minor in isolation, accrue over time to form powerful impressions. Whether we grew up with plenty, with scarcity, or with a volatile mixture of both, we internalised messages about what money is, what it means, and how it should be treated.

One of the most formative dimensions of early money socialisation is the way in which financial rules were communicated—or not communicated—within the family structure. Consider the simple institution of allowance. Some children receive a weekly stipend tied to chores, reinforcing the idea that money must be earned. Others are handed money as needed, sometimes inconsistently, which may cultivate entitlement or confusion around effort and reward. Still others receive nothing and are taught instead to make do or go without, encoding beliefs around unworthiness or financial invisibility. Each of these experiences seeds expectations and associations that often continue into adult life, dictating how we work, spend, save, and relate to financial systems.

Take the example of Leila, a successful project manager in her late thirties, who found herself compulsively tracking every penny and avoiding discretionary spending—even when well within her means. Through financial therapy, she uncovered that as a child, her requests for school supplies were often met with stress-fuelled lectures about budgeting and sacrifice. Although never overtly told that her needs were excessive, she absorbed the message that asking for money created tension and should be avoided. As an adult, her frugality wasn't about discipline—it was a protective mechanism designed to minimise the emotional risk she associated with financial requests.

Just as impactful are households where money is a source of conflict. Parental fights about spending, debt, or economic instability are not just momentary episodes; they become emotionally charged scripts. Children in such environments may come to associate money with stress, blame, or shame. These associations rarely dissolve with age. Instead, they often resurface in adulthood as financial anxiety, avoidance behaviours, or chronic under-earning. The adult may earn well yet feel inexplicably anxious when checking their account balance, or procrastinate on financial decisions as a way of sidestepping the emotional weight such decisions carry.

Moreover, many adults struggle with the effects of what psychologists call *scarcity trauma*. This does not only refer to extreme poverty or homelessness; it includes any formative experience where basic financial security was uncertain. Growing up in a household where electricity was periodically cut off, where meals were skipped, or where eviction notices were a familiar threat leaves a deep imprint on the nervous system. Neuroscience has demonstrated that chronic financial stress in childhood can activate the brain's stress response systems in enduring ways, leading to heightened anxiety, impaired decision-making, and difficulty with long-term planning.

One illustrative case is that of Roberto, a software engineer who developed obsessive saving habits, hoarding large sums in his account while neglecting his health, relationships, and professional development. Despite his outward success, Roberto lived with a persistent fear of financial collapse. This fear was not based on current reality but rooted in a childhood marked by frequent housing insecurity. In his words, "Every month felt like we were one missed rent payment away from disaster." Though those days were long past, his nervous system had never caught up. His scarcity mindset was not a flaw in character—it was a survival strategy that had outlived its usefulness.

The long-term consequences of childhood financial echoes are not limited to scarcity-based responses. Affluent upbringings can create their own challenges. Children raised in households where money was abundant but rarely discussed may emerge into adulthood with little financial literacy or a subconscious discomfort around earning. Others may internalise pressure to maintain a certain standard of living, not for personal fulfilment but as a means of preserving family status or avoiding perceived failure. The result can be a life that looks successful on paper but feels hollow, performative, or burdened by comparison.

To begin untangling these early influences, it is essential to move beyond analysis into conscious reflection. A useful practice is to engage in a structured memory inventory—an exercise in revisiting and reframing key financial moments from childhood. Begin by recalling a handful of specific memories involving money. These might include asking for something and being told no, witnessing a parent celebrate or worry over finances, receiving a gift that felt significant, or being given (or denied) access to financial information. For each memory, ask: What happened? How did I feel? What did I conclude about money from that experience? What did I conclude about myself in relation to money?

Patterns will often emerge. You may notice recurring themes—fear of not having enough, a sense of obligation to provide, a reluctance to depend on others, or discomfort with receiving. Recognising these themes is not about blaming caregivers, who themselves were often passing down inherited beliefs. Rather, it is about identifying the scripts you are still following so that you can decide whether they are still serving you. Like a homeowner discovering an old blueprint under the floorboards, you are not bound by it—but you cannot renovate what you do not first uncover.

It is also helpful to bring these reflections into conversation. Whether with a coach, therapist, or trusted peer, articulating your financial origin story can unlock insights that remain dormant in private rumination. Speaking these truths aloud often reveals the emotional charge they still carry and opens the door to conscious choice. In this way, reflection becomes a tool not only for awareness but for re-authoring. Once we locate the root of a belief, we can begin to question its validity and imagine more empowering alternatives.

Practical shifts often follow naturally from this inner work. Someone who recognises a tendency to under-earn rooted in early messages about humility may begin to advocate more confidently for fair compensation. A person who has long overcompensated for scarcity with overspending might find new satisfaction in simple pleasures, detached from performative consumption. These changes are not cosmetic. They represent deep recalibrations of identity and emotional association. And because they are anchored in lived awareness, they tend to be sustainable.

At a broader societal level, there is growing recognition of the importance of financial socialisation. Research in behavioural economics, developmental psychology, and even trauma studies increasingly supports what many have intuitively known: that money behaviours are not merely habits, but expressions of emotional history and psychological inheritance. This insight challenges the simplistic notion that financial success is purely a matter of discipline or education. It points instead to the need for integrated financial development—one that addresses both the cognitive and emotional dimensions of money.

Ultimately, the echoes of childhood do not dictate your financial destiny, but they do influence your default settings. By surfacing these echoes, examining their origins, and engaging with them consciously, you create space for a new financial narrative to emerge—one that is no longer dictated by the past but designed for the future you wish to build.

As you continue through this chapter and this book, let this subchapter serve as a foundation. Not a judgement, but a starting point. Your financial behaviours make sense in light of your experiences. They are adaptations, not flaws. And they can be updated. By tracing the lines back to childhood, you honour the roots of your financial identity while empowering yourself to grow beyond them. The story is still being written. You now hold the pen.

The Role of Financial Trauma

Money is often portrayed as a neutral tool—an objective medium of exchange, a measure of value, or a system of trade. Yet for many individuals, money is anything but neutral. It can be a source of dread, a trigger for shame, or a battlefield of conflicting emotions. While mainstream financial advice focuses heavily on strategy—

budgeting, saving, investing—what often goes unaddressed is the deeper emotional architecture that shapes how people relate to money in the first place. Among the most potent and overlooked of these psychological influences is financial trauma.

Financial trauma refers to the enduring psychological, emotional, and physiological consequences of distressing money-related experiences. These experiences may include chronic poverty, job loss, eviction, mounting debt, financial abuse, or repeated financial insecurity in childhood or adulthood. Unlike one-time financial setbacks, financial trauma leaves a lasting imprint. It activates the nervous system in ways similar to other forms of trauma, influencing a person's ability to make sound decisions, maintain stability, or even envision financial growth. Understanding the role of financial trauma is not just an exercise in empathy—it is essential for any meaningful financial transformation.

The nervous system is at the heart of this discussion. Neuroscientific research has shown that traumatic experiences, particularly those involving survival threats, bypass the logical centres of the brain and activate more primitive responses rooted in the amygdala and brainstem. These regions are responsible for initiating the "fight, flight, freeze, or fawn" reactions—defence mechanisms that prioritise immediate safety over long-term planning. When a person has experienced financial trauma, their nervous system can become sensitised to money-related stressors. A declined transaction, a surprise bill, or even the act of checking one's bank account can trigger a disproportionate sense of panic or paralysis.

For example, consider the case of Darren, a freelance illustrator who grew up in a household plagued by financial instability. As a child, he often overheard his parents arguing over missed rent and credit card debt. On more than one occasion, the electricity was shut off. As an adult, despite achieving relative financial success, Darren experienced extreme anxiety whenever he received large payments. Rather than feeling secure or accomplished, he felt overwhelmed. Without fully understanding why, he would often spend the money quickly or give it away. Therapy helped reveal that his nervous system had associated money with instability and impending loss. Holding onto it felt unsafe—like waiting for the other shoe to drop.

Darren's experience is not uncommon. For many, the nervous system's memory of financial trauma is more powerful than intellectual awareness. Rationally, they know they are not in immediate danger. Yet emotionally and physiologically, their body responds as if catastrophe is imminent. This incongruence can lead to a host of behaviours that seem irrational from the outside but are, in fact, adaptive survival strategies. These might include avoiding financial conversations, compulsive spending, excessive hoarding, or an inability to trust others with money.

Financial trauma also erodes a person's sense of agency. Repeated exposure to financial hardship can create what psychologists call *learned helplessness*—a condition where individuals begin to believe that no action they take can improve their situation. This belief often leads to disengagement. People stop opening bills, delay filing taxes, avoid checking their accounts, or decline opportunities that could elevate their financial position. The issue here is not laziness or irresponsibility; it is psychological fatigue. Constant vigilance, uncertainty, and stress deplete cognitive and emotional resources, making it harder to plan, persist, or hope.

Moreover, financial trauma is rarely experienced in isolation. It often intersects with other forms of marginalisation—racial inequality, gender-based pay gaps, health disparities, or disability. Research consistently shows that systemic barriers compound financial trauma, making recovery more complex and more urgent. For instance, Black and Indigenous communities in various parts of the world are disproportionately affected by generational wealth gaps, employment discrimination, and predatory lending practices. These external forces amplify the internal toll, embedding both societal and personal layers of trauma that cannot be addressed with spreadsheets alone.

This is where traditional budgeting advice falls short. Budgeting assumes a level of emotional safety and executive function that financial trauma often disrupts. It presumes a person can set realistic goals, delay gratification, and stick to a plan—abilities that require a regulated nervous system and a stable sense of self-worth. When those foundations are compromised, budgeting becomes not just ineffective, but sometimes re-traumatising. Being told to "just cut expenses" or "build an emergency fund" without acknowledging the psychological context can inadvertently reinforce shame and inadequacy.

What is needed instead is a framework for *money healing*. This approach recognises that financial transformation is not merely behavioural but deeply emotional and, in many cases, somatic. Healing begins by acknowledging that the body remembers what the mind may try to forget. It involves learning to recognise the signals of a dysregulated nervous system—tightness in the chest, rapid heartbeat, foggy thinking—during financial tasks. From there, techniques such as grounding exercises, breathwork, or somatic tracking can be employed to create a sense of safety in the body. This safety is not a luxury. It is a prerequisite for higher-order financial thinking.

Take the story of Priya, a small business owner who struggled with cash flow management. Every time she sat down to review her accounts, she experienced headaches, shallow breathing, and a sense of dread. Financial coaching helped her set up a basic accounting system, but the real shift came when she began incorporating mindfulness into her financial routine. Before opening her bank app, she would place a hand on her heart, take several deep breaths, and affirm that she was safe, even if the numbers were uncomfortable. Over time, this practice rewired her association with financial review—from a threat response to a moment of self-leadership.

Another critical aspect of money healing is *reframing*. Trauma distorts perception. It can lead individuals to misinterpret neutral events as dangerous or to overestimate the consequences of financial risk. Reframing involves questioning these distortions and replacing them with more balanced narratives. For example, the belief "I'll never get out of debt" can be reframed as "I've faced hardship before, and I'm learning new tools to manage my finances." This reframing process, supported by cognitive-behavioural therapy or guided journaling, can help interrupt the trauma loop and create space for hope.

Community support also plays a vital role. Trauma thrives in isolation but begins to dissolve in connection. Finding or creating safe spaces to talk about money—whether through financial therapy groups, community workshops, or peer networks—can reduce shame and normalise the emotional dimensions of finance. Hearing others articulate their struggles often helps individuals contextualise their own, transforming a solitary burden into a shared human experience. It is in this space of collective acknowledgement that new narratives and strategies can emerge.

Importantly, money healing is not about bypassing practical action. It is about sequencing it correctly. Rather than starting with budgeting or investing, individuals affected by financial trauma may need to begin with regulation—cultivating emotional and physiological stability in the presence of financial stressors. From that base, they can begin to make choices that are not reactive but intentional. Healing creates the internal conditions necessary for sustainable financial growth.

This healing process is also inherently non-linear. Just as trauma is cumulative, healing unfolds in layers. Progress may be followed by setbacks, confidence may give way to doubt, and success may surface unexpected emotions. This does not signal failure. It is part of the recalibration of the nervous system and identity. With patience and support, new patterns take hold—not through force, but through repetition, safety, and conscious engagement.

At a cultural level, recognising financial trauma invites a more compassionate and effective model of financial literacy. It challenges the myth that people who struggle with money simply lack discipline or intelligence. It repositions financial wellbeing not as a purely technical skill but as an integrative process involving mental health, emotional intelligence, social context, and self-awareness. This paradigm shift does not dilute financial responsibility—it enriches it. When people feel seen and supported in their full humanity, they are more likely to engage with their finances, take ownership of their choices, and build resilience over time.

Ultimately, addressing the role of financial trauma is not only a psychological necessity; it is an ethical one. If we want to create systems and societies that promote true financial inclusion, we must start by acknowledging the invisible wounds that distort financial agency. By integrating money healing into personal finance

education, coaching, and policy design, we create the conditions for deeper, more lasting transformation.

The truth is, many people are not just learning to budget—they are learning to feel safe. They are not just saving money—they are reclaiming their sense of control. And they are not just paying off debt—they are releasing the emotional residue of years spent in survival mode. This is the work of money healing. It is delicate, courageous, and profoundly human. And for those willing to engage with it, it opens the door not only to financial health, but to wholeness.

The Silent Influencers: Culture, Media, and Myths

When we examine our financial behaviours—how we earn, spend, save, or invest—we often look inward. We consider our upbringing, personal choices, and perhaps our psychological history. But to fully understand why we relate to money the way we do, we must also look outward. Culture, media, and myth play a profound, often invisible role in shaping our financial perceptions. These silent influencers do not operate in isolation; they are embedded in every advertisement, television plotline, social media feed, and political speech. They shape collective assumptions about wealth, morality, success, and identity. Without conscious scrutiny, they become the lens through which we view economic life—and, more crucially, ourselves.

Cultural narratives around money are among the most persistent and pervasive stories humans tell. In Western societies, for example, one of the most dominant scripts is the equation of money with power. Wealth is often portrayed as the ultimate form of agency—those who have money are presumed to have choice, voice, and impact. Conversely, those who lack financial resources are frequently cast as passive, dependent, or even morally inferior. These assumptions are not only inaccurate; they are deeply damaging. They perpetuate hierarchies of worth and subtly erode the self-esteem of those who struggle financially, suggesting that their situation is not just unfortunate but somehow deserved.

This belief system is reinforced through cultural mythologies that date back centuries. Consider the historical portrayal of wealth in religious and philosophical traditions. In some interpretations, prosperity is viewed as a sign of divine favour; in others, it is seen as a distraction from spiritual purity. The idea that "rich people are greedy" is not a contemporary creation—it has deep roots in cautionary tales and moral parables that equate abundance with excess and moral decay. While such narratives may have served historical purposes, they continue to inform modern attitudes, often subconsciously.

Contemporary media takes these narratives and amplifies them. The entertainment industry, in particular, traffics heavily in financial caricatures. The billionaire villain. The selfless pauper. The corrupt banker. The struggling artist. These characters are not just fictional—they become symbolic archetypes. Over time, they congeal into assumptions about what it means to be rich or poor, successful or struggling, worthy or not. A study conducted by the University of Southern California's Annenberg School for Communication found that in over 700 top-grossing films, wealthy characters were disproportionately portrayed as manipulative or disconnected from moral responsibility. While subtle, this messaging shapes our emotional responses. It's no surprise that many people feel a quiet discomfort with the idea of becoming wealthy themselves, fearing what it might make them—or how others might perceive them.

The rise of social media has added a new dimension to this distortion. Platforms like Instagram and TikTok often create financial illusions through curated lifestyles. Influencers stage luxury holidays, unbox high-end products, and showcase financial "hacks" without disclosing the real economics behind their posts—sponsorships, debt, or carefully engineered lighting. This creates an emotional dissonance. Viewers may feel inferior or anxious, wondering why their reality does not match the glittering façade they scroll through daily. The danger here is not just envy; it is miscalibration. When aspirational content replaces transparency, it warps our sense of what is normal, achievable, or necessary to be considered "successful."

Moreover, these media messages interact with existing cultural myths to produce contradictory expectations. We are encouraged to aspire to wealth, yet not to appear too comfortable with it. We are told to hustle, but also to be humble. Women, in particular, face a dual bind: encouraged to be financially independent, but often judged for being too ambitious or assertive when they pursue wealth. These conflicting signals create internal friction, often leading to self-sabotage or paralysis. The problem isn't simply that the messages exist—it's that we rarely pause to question their origins or accuracy.

To dismantle these internalised myths, the first step is to bring them into conscious awareness. What are the unspoken financial rules you've absorbed from your culture, community, or media consumption? Perhaps it's the belief that "money doesn't buy happiness," often used to rationalise staying in underpaid roles. Or the idea that "talking about money is rude," which discourages transparency in relationships and perpetuates inequity. These are not immutable truths. They are social constructs—learned and, therefore, unlearnable.

Real-world case studies illustrate the impact of such unexamined beliefs. Consider Maya, a high-achieving academic who consistently underpriced her consulting services. Despite her credentials and impact, she feared being seen as greedy or opportunistic. Her reluctance traced back to a cultural message she had internalised growing up: that education should be pursued for love of learning, not for financial gain. This belief had gone unchallenged for decades until a mentor invited her to consider the cost—not just to her, but to the communities she served—of remaining financially under-resourced. When Maya reframed her income not as self-indulgence but as sustainability, she was able to raise her rates without guilt, knowing that doing so allowed her to continue her mission from a place of strength rather than scarcity.

Such re-evaluations are not about abandoning values—they are about ensuring that inherited narratives are examined rather than accepted by default. Another example comes from Theo, a social worker raised in a faith tradition that viewed material wealth with suspicion. As he began building a successful coaching business, he found himself oscillating between pride and shame. It was only through dialogue with others who shared his background that he was able to contextualise those beliefs and adopt a more integrated view—one that honoured his values while embracing abundance as a means of service, not sin.

Practical tools can assist in this process of deconstruction. One such method is the media audit. Over the course of a week, keep a journal of every money-related message you encounter—television shows, articles, adverts, podcasts, even casual conversations. For each, note the implicit assumptions being made. Is wealth portrayed as virtuous or corrupting? Is financial struggle romanticised or pitied? Who is shown as financially competent—and who is not? Then reflect: which of these messages align with your lived experience and values? Which do not? This practice helps separate internal truth from external noise.

Another powerful approach is narrative replacement. Once you've identified a cultural myth that no longer serves you, craft a new narrative that does. If you were raised with the idea that "rich people don't care about others," consider counterexamples—philanthropists, ethical entrepreneurs, community leaders with wealth. Use these stories to reshape your internal associations. Over time, these revised narratives form the scaffolding for new behaviours, allowing you to pursue financial goals with greater integrity and fewer emotional roadblocks.

It is also vital to recognise the social justice dimensions of these narratives. Cultural myths about money are not just personal—they have political and economic implications. Myths that frame poverty as a personal failing rather than a systemic issue undermine support for social safety nets. Narratives that demonise wealth can discourage ethical people from accumulating the resources needed to drive change. In this context, auditing and reframing our money stories is not only an act of personal empowerment—it is a civic responsibility.

Ultimately, the silent influencers of culture, media, and myth will continue to shape the collective conversation around money. But you can choose whether to consume these messages passively or engage with them critically. Awareness is not about cynicism; it's

about discernment. When you see a wealthy character vilified on screen, you can ask what function that portrayal serves. When you hear a motivational speaker equating income with worth, you can interrogate the deeper values being sold. This mental clarity does more than protect you from manipulation—it helps you build a financial identity rooted in intentionality rather than inherited assumption.

Money, at its most fundamental level, is a human creation. And like all creations, its meaning is shaped by stories. The question is not whether we will be influenced by these stories—we already are. The question is whether we will allow them to go unchallenged. By naming the myths, decoding the media, and re-authoring our own narratives, we reclaim the power to define wealth on our own terms. Not as dictated by the silent influencers, but as articulated by the conscious self. That is the foundation upon which meaningful, sustainable financial wellbeing can truly be built.

Mapping Your Current Money Narrative

Every person has a money story. It is not simply a sequence of financial events or career milestones; it is the emotional and psychological narrative that weaves through each bank transaction, spending decision, and investment choice. This narrative influences how we earn, what we believe we deserve, how we respond to opportunity or risk, and whether we treat money as a tool of empowerment or a source of anxiety. Most crucially, it operates largely beneath the surface of our conscious awareness. Mapping your current money narrative is not just a reflective exercise—it is a vital diagnostic process that lays the foundation for meaningful transformation.

The concept of a "money narrative" draws from narrative psychology, which posits that individuals understand themselves through the stories they tell about their lives. These stories are not objective recollections; they are interpretive frameworks. In financial terms, this means we interpret past money experiences—be it receiving an inheritance, enduring a layoff, or growing up in a household with rigid spending rules—not as isolated incidents, but as part of an unfolding personal plot. The story we construct from these events becomes the script we follow. To change the outcome, we must first examine the script.

Consider Emily, a marketing consultant who consistently declined opportunities that would significantly increase her income. Despite her competence and drive, she described herself as someone who was "not great with money" and "not the kind of person who becomes wealthy." When she began exploring her financial history, she recalled a childhood marked by volatility: a father who made and lost fortunes with equal speed, and a mother who equated frugality with morality. Her internalised narrative became one of ambivalence: wealth was both desirable and dangerous, success admirable yet suspect. This narrative, although never explicitly stated, shaped her decisions—leading her to subconsciously avoid the very abundance she claimed to seek.

Mapping your money story requires a similar depth of self-inquiry. Begin by asking not what your financial outcomes are, but what story you believe about yourself in relation to money. Are you the scrappy survivor? The underdog? The responsible provider? The martyr? The lucky one? These roles, often inherited from family, culture, or past experiences, serve as anchors. They feel familiar, even when they are limiting. Naming these identities is the first step in gaining perspective over them.

To support this reflective process, it can be helpful to conduct a "financial story inventory"—a structured review of key money memories and the interpretations that accompanied them. Start by identifying significant financial milestones: your first paid job, a formative experience with debt or savings, a windfall, a major loss, or even a simple but emotionally charged memory, such as being denied a toy or witnessing a parent cry over bills. For each event, ask yourself: What happened? What emotions did I feel? What did I tell myself about money in that moment? And perhaps most importantly: What did I tell myself about *me* in that context?

The goal here is not to dwell on the past, but to extract the beliefs encoded within it. Often, these beliefs sound innocuous—"I have to work harder than everyone else," or "If I get too comfortable, I'll become complacent"—but they wield disproportionate influence over our choices. When these beliefs go unquestioned, they create patterns: habitual overspending, chronic under-earning, avoidance of financial planning, or a persistent sense that money is always just out of reach.

A compelling example of this process comes from Raj, a software developer who found himself oscillating between periods of high income and reckless spending. He initially framed this as poor discipline, but through narrative exploration, uncovered a deeper truth. As a child of immigrant parents who sacrificed much to provide for him, Raj internalised the idea that he should "enjoy what they couldn't." Subconsciously, he spent to honour their struggle—even when it led to financial instability. Once this narrative was made conscious, Raj was able to reframe his story: from one of reactive compensation to one of stewardship. He began making choices that honoured both his parents' sacrifice and his own long-term wellbeing.

This shift is what narrative psychologist Dan McAdams refers to as "narrative identity reconstruction"—the deliberate reshaping of one's self-story to accommodate growth, resilience, and purpose. It is not about erasing the past, but about re-authoring it. When applied to money, this means choosing to move from narratives of fear, scarcity, or shame to those of agency, clarity, and vision.

But transformation does not come from insight alone. It requires integration—embedding new narratives into daily financial behaviours. One way to begin this integration is by updating the language you use about money. Notice the metaphors and phrases that populate your inner dialogue: "I'm drowning in bills," "Money burns a hole in my pocket," "I'll never catch up." These are not just expressions—they are scripts reinforcing your story. Replacing them with conscious alternatives—"I'm prioritising what matters," "I'm learning to manage resources," "I'm designing my financial future"—begins to create new neural and emotional pathways.

Another tool for narrative integration is visualisation. Once you have identified the dominant themes of your current money story, imagine an alternative narrative. What if, instead of seeing yourself as the struggler, you envisioned yourself as the strategist? Instead of being the saver who never spends, what if you became the steward who balances enjoyment with planning? Crafting a new story allows your brain to rehearse different possibilities, priming it for new responses when familiar situations arise.

Of course, these practices require more than intellectual engagement—they require emotional honesty. Money narratives are rarely sterile. They are infused with grief, pride, longing, resentment, and sometimes trauma. To map your money story authentically, you must be willing to sit with these emotions, not bypass them. This process may evoke discomfort, but that discomfort is instructive. It signals the parts of your narrative that are ripe for revision.

It is also worth noting that money narratives are not static. They evolve as we do. Periodically revisiting your financial story allows you to identify when an old script is reasserting itself or when a new chapter is ready to be written. This dynamic engagement turns your money identity from a fixed label into a living document—a narrative you co-author with awareness and intention.

Moreover, this mapping process is not solely an individual endeavour. Our financial narratives are shaped in relationship—familial, romantic, social. Sharing aspects of your money story with a trusted partner or community can amplify clarity and accelerate growth. It disrupts the shame that often shrouds financial struggle and creates space for accountability, empathy, and collective learning.

In a broader sense, understanding and rewriting your money narrative is an act of self-leadership. It is a declaration that you will no longer be passively shaped by inherited assumptions, cultural myths, or outdated roles. It is a move from automation to authorship. The numbers on your account may be the output, but the story behind them is the engine.

As you engage with this exercise, remember: the purpose is not to craft a perfect narrative, but a conscious one. Perfection is static. Consciousness is adaptive. The more honest, curious, and intentional you are in mapping your current money identity, the more empowered you become to shape your financial future—not as a reaction to the past, but as an expression of your present values and vision.

You are not bound to the story you were given. You have the capacity—and the right—to write a new one. That story begins not with a bank statement, but with a mirror. Not with what you have, but with what you believe. And once belief is brought into awareness, it becomes a choice. And from choice, real change can emerge.

Chapter 2
Your Money Identity—Who Are You Financially?

Long before we're taught to track expenses or weigh the merits of compounding interest, we begin to form a sense of who we are in relation to money. And crucially, this identity is rarely a matter of conscious choice. Instead, it takes shape quietly—etched into us by the emotional climate of our childhood homes, the cultural signals we absorb without question, and the personal meanings we attach to words like success, scarcity, and enough. Curiously, many of us will devote time to monitoring budgets or perfecting spreadsheets, yet never stop to consider one of the most revealing questions in financial life: Who do I believe myself to be, financially?

This money identity is not simply a collection of habits or preferences—it's the emotional lens through which we experience wealth, work, and worth. It governs not only how we manage money, but how we perceive our own value in a world where money so often stands in as shorthand for status, safety, and legitimacy. The aim here is not to diagnose, label, or categorise. It is to observe. To understand. Because without this foundational clarity, the most sophisticated financial strategies tend to misfire. When your inner identity pulls in a different direction to your outer goals, self-sabotage isn't an anomaly—it's the inevitable outcome.

Traditional models often reduce people to tidy binaries: spender or saver, risk-lover or risk-avoider. But the human relationship with money is far messier than such simple divisions suggest. Instead, we turn to a more textured framework: money archetypes. These are recurring patterns of behaviour, deeply shaped by psychological imprints, that can offer insight into our emotional positioning around money. Think of "The Martyr Investor," who consistently overextends for others, neglecting their own financial needs. Or "The Guilty Earner," who, upon receiving a large payment, feels a creeping discomfort and soon finds themselves finding ways to give it away or lose it. Then there's "The Hoarding Minimalist," who cloaks themselves in austerity, not from pragmatism, but out of an ingrained belief that abundance is fleeting or unearned.

These archetypes aren't destiny. They're adaptive responses, forged in context—responses to pain, scarcity, or praise. Spotting your own dominant pattern isn't about pigeonholing yourself; it's about reclaiming a measure of freedom. You can't change what you can't see, but once you name it, you're no longer blindly following its script.

At the heart of this inquiry sits a deeper force: self-worth. Financially speaking, self-worth functions like a thermostat—it sets the temperature for what feels "normal" in terms of how much you earn, save, invest, or receive. And this isn't poetic licence; the link between self-worth and financial outcomes is backed by decades of research. People with healthy self-esteem are statistically more likely to negotiate salaries, take calculated risks, and persist when setbacks arise. Conversely, a low sense of worth shows up as chronic undercharging, an inability to receive, or an instinctive shrinking from financial visibility.

Take Tara—a qualified, experienced life coach who consistently underpriced her services. When challenged on it, she hesitated before admitting that raising her rates felt like overstepping. "Asking for too much," she said. But this wasn't a problem of pricing strategy—it was an echo of childhood beliefs. Raised in a home where money was framed as a zero-sum resource, she'd internalised the idea that wanting more was inherently selfish. Only by confronting and rewriting this internal story did she find the confidence to set rates aligned with her true value—an act that didn't just raise her income, but recalibrated her self-respect.

That misalignment between outer success and inner self-perception often manifests as financial imposter syndrome. Much like the classic professional variant, this phenomenon whispers that your achievements are flukes—that your wealth is accidental, temporary, or undeserved. It can affect anyone, regardless of income level. An executive may secretly fear exposure as incompetent. A first-generation wealth creator might feel alienated from their community, unsure whether their new status makes them a traitor or a fraud. These feelings, though often unspoken, exert powerful gravity over financial behaviour—driving avoidance, overcompensation, or retreat.

Often, these tensions don't announce themselves clearly. You'll find individuals who seem perfectly composed on the surface—decent salary, steady assets—while carrying deep, private undercurrents of guilt or shame. These emotions find ways to express themselves, usually through patterns we label as "sabotage." The term might sound severe, but the acts are disarmingly familiar: turning down promotions, spending impulsively after a period of discipline, dragging one's feet on taxes, walking away from a promising investment after the first hiccup. These aren't failures of willpower. They're expressions of cognitive dissonance. When your internal sense of self can't accommodate your external financial state, something eventually gives.

Consider Malik, a driven entrepreneur who landed a generous funding round for his business. Within half a year, most of it had been spent—lavish team hires, unnecessary services, an office upgrade that outpaced the company's needs. On the surface, it looked like overreach. But beneath that, Malik recognised something more complex. Raised in a household where money was always tight, his sense of self had been fused with struggle. The sudden influx of capital felt disorienting, even threatening. Without realising it, he was expelling the abundance just to return to a familiar psychological climate. Once this came into focus, he didn't just install budget controls—he did the deeper work of internalising stability as not just permissible, but natural.

And this brings us to the most hopeful point of the chapter: identity can be rewritten. You are not locked into your inherited script. But this re-authorship doesn't happen by accident. It requires attention. Intention. Begin by naming the role you currently occupy: Are you the over-functioning giver? The hesitant earner? The compulsive avoider? Then ask yourself—what would it mean to inhabit a new version of financial selfhood? Not just someone who earns more, but someone whose earning reflects confidence and alignment. Not just someone who invests wisely, but someone who trusts themselves to hold and grow value.

This isn't the terrain of shallow affirmations or airy vision boards. Real change lives in consistent practice. You might start by creating firmer boundaries around generosity, re-negotiating a long-stagnant rate, or establishing rituals—however small—that affirm your financial sovereignty. The emotional work is no less vital: therapy, journalling, finding communities where empowered financial identities are modelled and normalised. Gradually, the new narrative becomes less aspirational and more embodied. Not because you forced it, but because you built it, moment by moment, from the inside out.

Reworking your financial identity is neither a weekend task nor a linear one. It's a conversation—ongoing, occasionally messy—between the person you were shaped to be and the person you're now choosing to become. Through this lens, the money archetypes lose their rigidity and become tools. The shame-laced narratives around worth can be interrogated, not obeyed. The loops of sabotage begin to loosen, replaced by something steadier and kinder.

In the end, your financial self isn't just about pounds or pensions—it's about story. And the moment you realise you're the author of that story, everything changes. From reacting, you begin to design. That shift may be subtle, but its implications are vast. True wealth begins there—not simply in a fuller bank account, but in a clearer sense of self. And from that clarity, external change becomes not just more likely, but entirely possible.

Archetypes of Wealth and Worth

To understand a person's financial behaviour, it is not enough to track their transactions or study their savings rate. Behind every financial decision lies an internal framework—an emotional and psychological architecture built from past experiences, beliefs, and conditioned responses. This framework is rarely rational, often unconscious, and deeply tied to our sense of identity. One of the most effective ways to illuminate this inner terrain is through the lens of financial archetypes. Moving beyond the simplistic binary of "spender" versus "saver," archetypes offer a richer, more nuanced understanding of how individuals relate to money at the level of meaning, emotion, and self-worth.

Archetypes, in the Jungian tradition, are universal patterns of behaviour and motivation. In the context of money, these patterns shape how we earn, save, invest, give, and spend—not only in action, but in intention. They allow us to recognise ourselves in distinct yet overlapping roles, making the invisible aspects of our financial personality more legible. Identifying one's dominant archetype can be both revealing and transformative. It offers a mirror through which we can see our habits with fresh clarity and a framework for evolving them without shame or blame.

One such archetype is *The Martyr Investor*. This is the individual who prioritises the financial wellbeing of others to their own detriment. Often found among caregivers, nonprofit workers, or those with strong communal values, the Martyr Investor sees money as a tool of service—but struggles to include themselves in the equation of that service. They may consistently give to family members, undercharge for their work, or neglect retirement savings in favour of more immediate support for others. On the surface, this behaviour appears noble. But over time, it can lead to burnout, resentment, or a sense of personal depletion. The underlying belief here is that personal financial security must be sacrificed for moral integrity—a belief often rooted in early socialisation or religious values that frame wealth as inherently selfish.

Consider Angela, a therapist who worked primarily with low-income clients. Despite increasing demand for her services, she resisted raising her rates. When her own finances became strained, she continued working long hours rather than seeking more balanced solutions. In therapy, Angela revealed that she associated higher fees with abandonment—mirroring a childhood fear that support is conditional and fleeting. Recognising her Martyr Investor archetype allowed her to reframe her professional ethos. She began offering a sliding scale with limits, ensuring she could support others without undermining herself. By integrating sustainability into her definition of service, Angela honoured both her clients and her own financial integrity.

Another common archetype is *The Guilty Earner*. This person earns well but feels uncomfortable holding on to money. They may downplay their success, give away bonuses, or spend impulsively after a financial win. The core issue here is not extravagance, but unworthiness. The Guilty Earner struggles to reconcile their financial gains with their internalised self-image or community values. This is especially prevalent among individuals who have experienced upward mobility—first-generation professionals, immigrants, or those who grew up in environments of scarcity. For them, wealth can feel disloyal, indulgent, or isolating.

Take Marcus, a tech executive from a working-class background. Despite earning a seven-figure salary, he lived with a constant undercurrent of anxiety and guilt. He avoided discussing money with his family, felt uneasy around friends from his old neighbourhood, and regularly donated large sums without strategy or sustainability. At the root was a belief that financial comfort meant abandoning his roots. By naming his archetype, Marcus began to explore more nuanced ways of staying connected—investing in community projects, having open conversations with family about money, and embracing the idea that wealth could be a bridge, not a betrayal.

Then there is *The Hoarding Minimalist.* This archetype finds comfort in control. They equate financial security with self-denial, viewing spending as risky and abundance as fleeting. They may live far below their means, obsess over budgeting, and feel uneasy making financial decisions that involve risk or pleasure. While outwardly disciplined, the Hoarding Minimalist often operates from fear rather than empowerment. Their minimalism is not a conscious lifestyle choice, but a defensive posture. The belief anchoring this archetype is that stability is only achievable through rigid constraint.

Priya, a civil engineer, exemplified this archetype. Despite a stable job and ample savings, she hesitated to take holidays, upgrade her ageing car, or invest in personal development. Her fear of a financial downturn was disproportionate to her actual circumstances. Through coaching, she uncovered memories of her family losing their home during her adolescence. Although that crisis was decades behind her, the emotional memory remained active. By addressing the trauma behind her behaviours, Priya was able to shift from fear-based frugality to intentional minimalism, choosing where to allocate resources in alignment with her values—not as a reaction to a long-past threat.

These archetypes are not pathologies. They are adaptations. They emerge in response to our environments, shaped by necessity, emotion, and social influence. Nor are they mutually exclusive. Most individuals embody a blend of archetypes, with one or two dominant patterns. What matters is not to fix or eliminate these tendencies, but to understand them. Archetypes offer a language for our financial psyche—a way to name the invisible drivers behind our behaviours.

Understanding your archetype also has practical implications. It informs how you set goals, how you make decisions under pressure, how you experience financial success or failure. For example, a Martyr Investor might need to build boundaries around giving. A Guilty Earner may benefit from affirmations that decouple worth from guilt. A Hoarding Minimalist could experiment with planned indulgences to recalibrate their nervous system. These are not indulgent exercises—they are essential recalibrations that support financial resilience and psychological well-being.

Moreover, recognising your archetype can radically shift the way you interact with financial education. Much of mainstream financial advice is designed with a presumed archetype in mind—often a Rational Planner, someone who makes decisions free from emotional influence. But this is rarely the case. Most people, even when financially literate, behave irrationally at times because they are not driven by logic alone. They are driven by identity. When advice ignores this, it fails to resonate. When advice is tailored to archetypal patterns, it becomes transformative.

It is equally important to acknowledge how these archetypes intersect with cultural, gendered, and socioeconomic narratives. The Guilty Earner may be more prevalent among women who have been socially conditioned to prioritise caregiving over accumulation. The Hoarding Minimalist may be amplified in communities with a history of economic marginalisation. The Martyr Investor may arise from traditions that equate service with sacrifice. Understanding these contextual layers deepens our compassion—for ourselves and others—and prevents us from misinterpreting deeply rational protective behaviours as mere financial missteps.

Ultimately, financial archetypes are not cages—they are keys. They unlock deeper understanding, offering us the insight needed to change not only what we do with money, but how we *feel* about those actions. They reveal that beneath every budget line is a belief, and behind every belief is a story. And while we may not have written the opening chapters, we do have the power to edit the script.

To work with your archetype is to engage in conscious self-leadership. It is to bring compassion to patterns that once felt confusing or frustrating. It is to reclaim choice where there was once only reaction. And perhaps most importantly, it is to build a financial life that reflects who you *really* are—not who you were conditioned to be.

As you move through this chapter, allow these archetypes to serve not as final definitions, but as starting points. Use them to map your emotional relationship with wealth, your inherited beliefs about worth, and your behavioural tendencies under financial pressure. By naming the pattern, you begin to release its hold. And from that clarity, you can begin to craft a new identity—one rooted not in fear, guilt, or scarcity, but in purpose, confidence, and agency. That is the power of financial self-awareness. It doesn't merely change your behaviour. It changes your story. And from that story, a different kind of wealth can emerge—one that reflects not only how much you have, but how deeply you know yourself.

The Mirror of Self-Worth

Money does not exist in a vacuum. It is not merely a neutral tool of exchange or a rational system of inputs and outputs. It is, in many respects, a mirror—one that reflects not just our financial acumen but our internal sense of worth. Behind every pay negotiation declined, every investment postponed, every opportunity bypassed, and every savings goal abandoned, there is often a hidden undercurrent: a quiet belief about what we deserve. And this belief, more than any spreadsheet or market trend, governs the upper limit of our financial potential.

Self-worth is the internal measure of how valuable we perceive ourselves to be—not only in the eyes of others, but within our own psychological landscape. It informs our confidence in professional settings, our ability to set boundaries, and our sense of entitlement to resources, rest, abundance, and joy. In financial terms, self-worth operates like a thermostat. It regulates the income we allow ourselves to pursue, the prices we feel comfortable setting, the risks we are willing to take, and the boundaries we maintain around money. When self-worth is low, we tend to earn, save, and invest less—not due to incompetence, but due to a mismatch between what we desire and what we believe we are permitted to have.

The link between self-worth and financial behaviour is well established in both psychological and economic research. Studies have shown that individuals with lower self-esteem are less likely to negotiate salaries, more likely to undercharge for their services, and often more prone to financial self-sabotage. In contrast, those with a healthy sense of self-worth tend to display greater financial initiative, resilience, and clarity. But it is not simply a matter of external confidence; it is a matter of internal permission.

Take the case of Elena, a freelance interior designer who, despite her growing portfolio and steady stream of clients, consistently charged less than her industry peers. When asked why she hadn't raised her rates, she hesitated: "I guess I just don't feel like I'm there yet." "There," of course, was not a measurable place. It was an emotional threshold—a sense of enoughness that had nothing to do with her skill or results. When she traced this feeling back, Elena recalled being told as a child to "be grateful for whatever you get" and that "asking for more is selfish." These well-intentioned lessons had calcified into adult beliefs that made financial ambition feel inappropriate. Her rates were not a business strategy. They were a reflection of an identity silently shaped by early narratives of modesty and guilt.

Such dynamics are not unique to entrepreneurs. In the corporate world, self-worth is equally influential. Research by Linda Babcock and Sara Laschever in *Women Don't Ask* reveals that men initiate salary negotiations four times more often than women, and when they do, they typically ask for—and receive—higher amounts. While structural inequalities undoubtedly play a role, the researchers also point to internalised beliefs about worthiness and permission. If you don't believe you are worth more, you are far less likely to ask for it, let alone insist on it. And this pattern repeats itself not just in salaries, but in bonuses, promotions, investment decisions, and business deals.

The internal dialogue is often subtle but persistent: *Who am I to ask for more? What if they say no? What if I can't deliver?* These questions are rarely rooted in actual performance. They stem from a deeper sense of self-evaluation—an internal scoring system that keeps us tethered to familiar limits. Even when success is achieved, those with shaky self-worth may find themselves uncomfortable with the rewards, seeking to diminish, deflect, or give them away.

This is the emotional architecture of what psychologist Gay Hendricks terms "The Upper Limit Problem." When individuals surpass their internalised threshold for success, joy, or wealth, they often unconsciously create conflict or setbacks to restore equilibrium. This phenomenon is visible in those who receive a bonus and immediately overspend, entrepreneurs who sabotage promising deals, or professionals who burn out after achieving a long-sought milestone. The issue is not lack of desire, but internal dissonance. The outer reality has changed, but the inner self-concept has not.

Addressing this dissonance requires more than external validation or behavioural hacks. It calls for a conscious inquiry into the roots of self-worth. Where did your beliefs about deservingness come from? Were you praised for effort or perfection? Did your caregivers model financial confidence or chronic worry? Were you taught that money was a reward for goodness, or a source of corruption? These early imprints are not just childhood memories—they are the foundation upon which our adult financial identities are built.

Take Jamal, a financial analyst from a working-class background, who was recently promoted to a senior role. With the promotion came a substantial salary increase and visibility in his firm. Instead of celebrating, he found himself plagued by self-doubt and imposter syndrome. He hesitated to speak up in meetings, turned down opportunities to lead, and even questioned whether the promotion was a clerical error. Jamal's discomfort was not due to a lack of skill—it stemmed from an internalised belief that people like him were not meant to be in positions of financial or professional power. He was trying to live a new financial life with an outdated identity.

Through coaching and self-reflection, Jamal began to explore the disconnect. He wrote letters to his younger self, unpacked the messages he had absorbed about class and competence, and slowly began to affirm a new narrative. As his self-worth recalibrated, so too did his behaviours. He began taking bolder decisions, investing in his own development, and eventually mentoring others facing similar transitions. His story illustrates a crucial truth: when our sense of worth expands, our financial life follows.

This inner recalibration is not merely psychological—it has behavioural implications. When self-worth is aligned with ambition, individuals are more likely to invest in themselves. They view education, mentorship, wellness, and rest not as luxuries, but as necessities. They are more likely to say no to underpaid opportunities, to assert their value, and to protect their time and energy. These behaviours are not ego-driven; they are rooted in a stable internal foundation that says, "I am enough, and I deserve to live from that place."

For those looking to strengthen their financial self-worth, practical strategies can support the internal shift. One approach is the "evidence inventory"—a journaling practice in which individuals list tangible proof of their competence, impact, and growth. Over time, this list becomes a counterweight to the inner critic. Another strategy is the "value ladder"—a reflection on how your work or presence creates value at multiple levels, from personal to societal. By articulating your contribution clearly, you begin to internalise it.

It is also essential to revisit and challenge limiting beliefs. If you catch yourself thinking, "I'm not good with money," or "People like me don't become wealthy," ask yourself: Whose voice is that? When did I first hear it? Is it objectively true—or emotionally familiar? Replace these beliefs with ones that are not only empowering, but credible. Self-worth grows not from delusion, but from honest self-recognition.

Ultimately, the mirror of self-worth reflects not just what we think about money, but what we believe about ourselves. It asks us to consider whether our financial limitations are circumstantial—or self-imposed. It challenges the idea that strategy alone is sufficient for transformation. And it invites us to imagine what might be possible if we stopped waiting to be "ready," and instead decided to be worthy now.

The truth is, you will never outperform your self-concept for long. You may get lucky, hustle hard, or find temporary success—but if your internal thermostat is set to lack or unworthiness, you will eventually cool your environment to match. Lasting change happens when your identity catches up with your goals, when you stop asking for permission to earn, save, and invest well—and begin acting from the belief that you already deserve to.

Self-worth is not arrogance. It is the quiet certainty that you have value, and that your financial life should reflect that value in tangible ways. It is the foundation upon which sustainable wealth is built—not just wealth in numbers, but wealth in confidence, peace, and possibility. When you meet your reflection in the financial mirror, what do you see? More importantly, what do you believe you're worth? The answer to that question will shape everything that follows.

Financial Imposter Syndrome

For many, financial success does not bring the expected feelings of safety, confidence, or fulfilment. Instead, it brings discomfort, anxiety, or a gnawing sense that it's all undeserved—that any moment now, someone might realise they don't belong. This phenomenon, commonly referred to as *financial imposter syndrome*, is more than a fleeting insecurity. It is a deep-rooted psychological experience that distorts how individuals perceive their achievements and their right to enjoy or sustain financial stability. Even when external indicators suggest prosperity, the internal narrative whispers a different story: *You're not meant to have this.*

Imposter syndrome, as a psychological concept, was first identified in 1978 by psychologists Pauline Clance and Suzanne Imes, who observed it predominantly in high-achieving women. Though originally discussed in the context of academic and professional environments, its financial manifestation is equally prevalent—and arguably more insidious. Financial imposter syndrome is not simply about doubting one's career competence; it's about feeling emotionally and psychologically disconnected from one's financial reality, regardless of how it was earned. It is the internalisation of unworthiness in the face of evidence to the contrary.

This disconnect is particularly pronounced among those who experience rapid financial growth, upward social mobility, or a significant shift in economic identity. First-generation wealth builders, immigrants, freelancers entering new income brackets, or individuals who've overcome poverty are especially vulnerable. They often carry psychological and cultural scripts that equate money with moral compromise, social betrayal, or emotional distance. When these internalised scripts clash with newfound financial success, cognitive dissonance emerges. Instead of integrating wealth as part of a healthy self-concept, they feel like actors on a borrowed stage.

Consider the story of Daniel, a software developer raised in a working-class family in Manchester. After several promotions, Daniel found himself earning more in a year than his parents had in five. Although proud on the surface, he privately battled with guilt, anxiety, and a persistent sense that he had "gotten lucky." He avoided investing, was reluctant to spend on himself, and constantly feared that one misstep would unravel everything. When asked about his financial plans, he deflected with humour or minimised his accomplishments. Daniel wasn't experiencing a lack of financial competence; he was struggling to reconcile who he had become with who he used to be.

Such experiences are not merely emotional—they are neurologically reinforced. The human brain thrives on consistency and familiarity. When reality changes rapidly—especially for the better—it can trigger the amygdala's threat response. The subconscious mind, conditioned by years of scarcity or caution, does not distinguish between a threat to physical safety and a perceived threat to identity. In other words, wealth can feel emotionally unsafe if one's internal belief system has not evolved to accommodate it.

Moreover, social context often exacerbates the discomfort. Financial imposter syndrome does not exist in a vacuum—it is shaped by relationships and cultural norms. Someone who grows up in a financially modest community and later enters a high-income circle may feel caught between worlds, unsure of how to relate to either. They may be perceived as "too rich" by their family or "too frugal" by their new peers. This identity tension is compounded when language around money remains emotionally loaded. Phrases like "selling out," "getting above yourself," or "money changes people" serve to reinforce the idea that financial success is incompatible with authenticity or loyalty.

In women, these experiences are often magnified by gendered conditioning. Cultural messaging frequently teaches women to associate care, humility, and selflessness with virtue. As a result, women may internalise the belief that seeking wealth is unfeminine, selfish, or socially dangerous. Even when they achieve financial milestones, they may downplay them, deflect praise, or self-sabotage. A study by Allianz found that 57% of women feel overwhelmed by financial planning, and many attribute their discomfort not to lack of knowledge but to feelings of inadequacy or imposture. This suggests that the issue is not education—it is identity.

The corporate world is not immune. Executives, lawyers, and entrepreneurs regularly report feeling like financial imposters, especially when they come from non-traditional backgrounds or enter elite spaces without generational wealth. Despite accolades and earnings, they carry a chronic fear of being "found out"—a fear that often leads to overworking, under-asking, or chronic underinvestment in themselves. The irony is stark: those who most doubt their financial legitimacy are often the ones who have earned it through extraordinary resilience and effort.

Financial imposter syndrome also shapes how people behave with money. Those afflicted may avoid financial planning, resist advice, or fail to take advantage of wealth-building opportunities—not because they lack the capacity, but because they feel undeserving. This can lead to a self-perpetuating cycle. Avoidance leads to poor decisions, which reinforces feelings of inadequacy, which leads to further avoidance. Over time, this pattern becomes entrenched, not as a matter of knowledge, but of narrative.

So, what does it take to break the cycle? The first step is recognition. Naming the phenomenon creates a pause between belief and behaviour. It allows individuals to observe their thoughts with distance and curiosity. Instead of accepting the narrative—*I don't belong here*—they can begin to ask, *Where did this belief come from? Is it based on evidence or emotion? Is it serving me or holding me back?*

From there, reframing becomes essential. Financial success must be seen not as an aberration but as a continuation—a result of choices, efforts, and capacities that are real and replicable. This reframing is not about blind affirmation; it is about contextualising success within a narrative of growth, rather than exception. It may involve revisiting past accomplishments, identifying personal strengths, and anchoring financial outcomes to consistent effort rather than luck.

Journaling can be a powerful tool in this process. One exercise involves writing two parallel stories: the one your imposter voice tells, and the one grounded in fact. For example, "I just got lucky with that promotion" can be rewritten as "I was chosen for promotion because I consistently delivered value and took initiative." The act of writing reframes the subconscious narrative, gradually building a new internal script.

It is also critical to foster environments that validate this growth. Sharing imposter feelings with trusted peers or mentors often reveals how common they are. Normalising these experiences diminishes their power. Support groups, professional coaching, and financial therapy can offer further reinforcement, providing both cognitive strategies and emotional safety to explore difficult beliefs.

Practical financial planning also plays a role in resolving imposter dynamics. Developing a long-term financial strategy, no matter how simple, creates a sense of control and coherence. It signals to the brain that wealth is not accidental—it is managed, sustained, and worthy of care. Celebrating financial wins, however modest, reinforces the idea that success is deserved. It builds what psychologists call "earned confidence"—a sense of self-trust grounded in repeated action.

Importantly, those who struggle with financial imposter syndrome must learn to update their self-image. Our identities tend to lag behind our realities. It is not unusual to have reached a new level of success while still feeling like the person who struggled to get by. But as with any transition, integration takes time. Being wealthy, or even financially stable, is not a betrayal of who you were—it is an evolution of who you are becoming. And that evolution does not require the abandonment of values, but the expansion of them.

At its core, financial imposter syndrome is not about numbers. It is about belonging. It is about reconciling financial visibility with psychological safety, abundance with authenticity, and growth with groundedness. By addressing the emotional root, rather than just the behavioural symptom, we can move from insecurity to integrity—from feeling like an imposter to becoming the rightful architect of our financial lives.

The work is not always comfortable, but it is deeply necessary. For as long as your wealth feels like a costume, you will live in fear of being unmasked. But when it becomes an extension of who you are—honestly earned, wisely stewarded, and consciously received—it can finally serve its true purpose: not to impress, not to protect, but to empower. You are not an accident. Neither is your success. The sooner you believe that, the more fully you can claim everything you've already built—and everything still to come.

Self-Sabotage: When You Burn the Bag

There is a paradox at the heart of modern finance: while many people outwardly desire greater financial freedom—higher earnings, secure investments, long-term wealth—an astonishing number actively undermine their own progress when these opportunities materialise. This self-sabotage is not always dramatic. It can be as subtle as declining a raise out of discomfort, overspending after a bonus, or indefinitely postponing investment decisions with a litany of rational justifications. It may present as poor planning or indifference, but beneath the surface lies something more complex:

a psychological resistance to having, keeping, or growing wealth. When people "burn the bag"—that is, destroy or diminish their own financial gains—they are not merely making bad decisions. They are acting out unresolved emotional scripts where behavioural finance and psychological therapy intersect.

To understand why self-sabotage is so pervasive, we must first move beyond the assumption that financial decisions are purely rational. Classical economics posits the individual as a logical actor who evaluates costs and benefits before making optimal choices. But behavioural finance—an interdisciplinary field blending psychology, economics, and cognitive science—has dismantled this ideal. Human beings are anything but consistently rational, especially when money touches on deeper emotional territories such as identity, security, shame, or self-worth.

A key insight from behavioural finance is that people do not simply manage money—they manage emotion through money. Spending, saving, investing, or avoiding are not just financial acts; they are emotional expressions. Sometimes these expressions are healthy—such as using savings to create future security. But often, especially when unexamined, they can become forms of self-sabotage. This is particularly evident when individuals receive financial windfalls. Unexpected gains—a tax refund, inheritance, bonus, or lottery win—often trigger internal conflict. Without a strong, stable internal framework for holding wealth, recipients may unconsciously find ways to rid themselves of the money as quickly as possible.

Consider the case of Ryan, a marketing consultant who received a sizeable payout after the sale of his start-up. Within eighteen months, he had drained nearly the entire amount through lavish spending, poor investments, and generosity that bordered on compulsive. When asked about it, he admitted, "It never felt like it was mine." Ryan's behaviour was not a matter of ignorance—he had access to advisors and had read extensively on financial literacy. But intellectually knowing how to manage money is not the same as being psychologically prepared to hold it. Ryan's identity had not caught up to his new financial status. Deep down, he still saw himself as the underdog—scrappy, overlooked, never fully secure. Wealth disrupted that identity, and his subconscious corrected the imbalance.

This pattern is not uncommon. The phenomenon of "sudden wealth syndrome" is well-documented among lottery winners and athletes who experience rapid financial gains. Studies have shown that within three to five years, a significant percentage of lottery winners return to their previous financial state or worse. The reason is rarely technical mismanagement alone; it is emotional dysregulation. When money arrives faster than identity evolves, sabotage becomes a form of equilibrium restoration.

Self-sabotage also appears in more subtle, everyday forms. Take Maya, an academic who consistently declined salary negotiations despite her growing responsibilities. Her rationale was that asking for more might make her appear ungrateful. But beneath that was an unspoken belief that more money would alienate her from her peers or make her complicit in systems she had long critiqued. Her discomfort was not with money per se, but with the perceived moral implications of abundance. In her mind, modesty equalled integrity. This internalised equation kept her financially stagnant, despite objective evidence that she was undervalued.

Or consider Kevin, a self-employed graphic designer who avoided investing entirely, despite having significant savings. His excuse was always timing: the market was volatile, the fees were unclear, the risk was too high. But his hesitance persisted across years and economic cycles. Eventually, through coaching, he unearthed an early memory of watching his father lose money in a failed business venture. The trauma of that event had implanted a belief that wealth accumulation invited loss. For Kevin, not investing was not poor strategy—it was self-protection.

These examples reveal that self-sabotage is not a flaw in discipline; it is a manifestation of unexamined belief systems. These beliefs are often formed early and reinforced subtly: that wanting more is greedy, that wealth corrupts, that financial comfort will create distance in relationships, that success will trigger backlash or abandonment. Such beliefs rarely announce themselves. They operate in the background, quietly guiding decisions, stoking guilt, or rationalising avoidance.

The intersection between behavioural finance and therapy becomes essential here. Traditional financial advice—budget, save, invest—is ineffective when it ignores the emotional drivers of decision-making. A financial plan may be technically sound, but if it does not account for the client's psychological comfort with money, it is unlikely to be executed. Therapists, on the other hand, have historically been slow to integrate financial issues into psychological work, despite their centrality to clients' wellbeing. The emerging field of financial therapy seeks to bridge this gap, offering an integrated approach that treats financial behaviour as both a practical and emotional matter.

At its core, financial self-sabotage is a misalignment between behaviour and belief. It is the attempt to live a financially abundant life with a scarcity-conditioned mindset. Until this mindset is addressed, efforts at behavioural change are temporary. This is where practices such as money journaling, inner narrative mapping, and emotional regulation techniques become indispensable. They allow individuals to surface the beliefs driving their behaviour and begin the work of reframing them.

For example, a useful exercise involves tracking not just financial decisions, but the emotions surrounding them. What were you feeling when you made that unplanned purchase? What thought preceded your decision to ignore your investment account for six months? What story played in your head when you said no to a raise? Over time, patterns emerge—not of carelessness, but of unspoken fears, inherited guilt, or unresolved trauma. Bringing these patterns to light is not about blame—it is about choice. You cannot change what you do not see.

Equally important is expanding one's identity to include financial stability and growth. This involves deliberately imagining a self who handles wealth with clarity, ease, and purpose. Visualisation, affirmation, and narrative rewriting are not magic—they are psychological conditioning tools. When the nervous system is habituated to scarcity or chaos, these practices serve to rewire emotional responses and normalise new experiences.

Community and environment also play a powerful role. If everyone in your circle struggles financially or demonises success, it becomes difficult to sustain growth without triggering internal conflict. Surrounding oneself with financially empowered peers, mentors, or communities helps recalibrate what is seen as "normal." It provides both support and modelling for healthier behaviour.

There is also a case for structural interventions. Automating savings, investing incrementally, or setting up financial guardrails can help counteract impulsive behaviours while deeper work is underway. These systems act as temporary stabilisers—protecting individuals from their own tendencies until their internal world aligns with their external goals.

Ultimately, financial self-sabotage is not a character defect. It is a signal. A signal that your financial life has outgrown your current psychological framework. That your identity, shaped by past limitations, is now being asked to expand. It is uncomfortable, yes—but it is also the moment of transformation. When you feel the impulse to burn the bag, to undo your own progress, to slip back into old patterns—pause. Ask not what you are doing, but what you are defending. Often, the answer will surprise you.

Transformation does not begin with spreadsheets or slogans. It begins with the courage to look within, to question the familiar, and to write a new narrative—one in which success is not feared, sabotaged, or apologised for, but received with grace, sustained with intention, and used with wisdom. When we stop burning the bag, we stop fearing our own power. And in that space, a different kind of wealth becomes possible—not just financial, but personal, relational, and deeply, lastingly liberating.

Rewriting Your Wealth Identity

The most powerful shifts in financial life rarely begin in a spreadsheet—they begin in the self-concept. Long before a person sets a budget, negotiates a raise, or makes an investment, they carry a set of beliefs and internalised narratives that determine what they will allow themselves to have, hold, or grow. This internal framework, often unconscious, shapes the architecture of our financial decisions. It is what behavioural psychologists refer to as *identity-based behaviour*: we act not in accordance with logic alone, but with who we believe ourselves to be. To create lasting transformation, we must therefore confront a central question—*Who are you financially?* And, more importantly, *Who are you willing to become?*

Rewriting your wealth identity is the process of consciously reshaping your financial self-concept. It is not about pretending to be someone you are not; it is about realigning your actions with a more accurate, empowered, and expansive version of who you are. This process integrates insights from psychology, behavioural finance, and narrative theory, revealing that wealth is not simply something you acquire—it is something you learn to embody.

For many, their current wealth identity was not consciously chosen. It emerged through accumulated experiences: growing up in environments where money was scarce or taboo; witnessing family dynamics shaped by sacrifice or overindulgence; absorbing cultural messages that linked wealth to greed, danger, or disconnection. These early inputs crystallise into archetypes—the over-giver, the under-earner, the avoidant planner—and begin to operate as default settings. They form an invisible ceiling, governing the upper limit of what we allow ourselves to earn, keep, and feel safe with.

Consider Leanne, a freelance writer who, despite consistent demand for her work, never raised her rates. Her peers encouraged her to charge more, and her clients routinely praised her output. Yet something held her back. Through coaching, she traced the discomfort to childhood memories of her mother working multiple jobs yet insisting that "good people don't charge too much." Leanne's identity was shaped not only by economic behaviour but by emotional allegiance. Her hesitation was not about market dynamics—it was about loyalty to inherited beliefs. Rewriting her wealth identity required not only economic strategy but emotional reconciliation.

The act of rewriting begins with awareness. You cannot alter what you haven't named. Start by examining your current financial behaviours with curiosity. Do you undercharge, overspend, delay decisions, or defer to others on money matters? Rather than judging these behaviours, treat them as data points. Each pattern is a clue pointing to an underlying identity. If you frequently delay investing, perhaps you don't see yourself as "someone who builds wealth." If you find it difficult to receive financial praise, perhaps your internal narrative says that success is dangerous or undeserved. These are not random patterns—they are the outward expression of inward definitions.

Once patterns are identified, the next step is to interrogate the narratives behind them. This is where psychology meets narrative reframing. Ask yourself: *Whose voice is this? When did I first hear it? Does it still serve me?* Often, our financial identities are built from scripts written by others—parents, teachers, peers, media. They served a function at the time, offering safety, approval, or belonging. But as we grow, these scripts can become outdated, even obstructive. The child who learned to be invisible to avoid criticism may become the adult who undercharges to avoid conflict. The teenager who associated wealth with arrogance may become the entrepreneur who avoids visibility to protect their humility.

These inherited narratives can be rewritten through deliberate, consistent re-authoring. This involves developing a new internal story—one that reflects not only who you are but who you are becoming. Crucially, this story must feel emotionally resonant and intellectually credible. Overly positive affirmations that feel disconnected from reality often trigger resistance rather than change. Instead of declaring, "I am a millionaire," someone might start with, "I am learning to build a sustainable financial life with clarity and confidence." This reframing is both more believable and more supportive of identity expansion.

Real-world rituals can reinforce this shift. Tasha, a mid-career executive, used daily journaling to build a relationship with her new wealth identity. Each morning, she wrote three sentences about the kind of financial leader she was becoming. These included tangible actions ("I review my accounts weekly with confidence") and emotional states ("I feel safe earning more than I need"). Over time, this practice moved her from conceptual agreement to embodied belief. Her behaviour shifted as well—she began investing more strategically, renegotiated her contract, and made her first real estate investment. The journaling had not created financial success, but it had paved the path for her to receive it fully.

Language plays a critical role in this transformation. The words we use to describe ourselves, our finances, and our possibilities shape the neural pathways that govern action. Notice how often you say things like "I'm terrible with money," "I just can't save," or "I'm not one of those investor types." These are not merely descriptive statements; they are identity declarations. Rewriting them, both internally and aloud, is not delusional—it is foundational. Language is the code of identity, and changing it requires repetition, awareness, and conscious replacement.

Another important dimension of wealth identity is the emotional range we allow ourselves to experience in relation to money. Many people equate financial abundance with stress, guilt, or alienation. As a result, they resist financial expansion, not because they lack ambition, but because they associate growth with emotional loss. Rewriting wealth identity means expanding your emotional tolerance for having, receiving, and holding wealth—not with detachment, but with grace. This includes learning to feel joy without guilt, confidence without arrogance, and generosity without depletion.

It also requires a community context. Identity is reinforced socially. If your environment is filled with people who echo your old beliefs—those who scoff at wealth, fear ambition, or equate financial literacy with elitism—it becomes difficult to sustain a new identity. Seek out mentors, communities, and peer groups that reflect your evolving self-concept. Their presence acts as a mirror, reflecting back what is possible and reinforcing what is emerging. This does not mean abandoning your roots or rejecting those who shaped you. It means honouring your growth by choosing environments that support it.

Critically, rewriting your wealth identity is not about becoming someone you are not. It is about reclaiming parts of yourself that have been buried under layers of conditioning, fear, or obligation. It is about returning to the truth that your value is not contingent on scarcity, that your desires are not inherently selfish, and that your financial life can be an expression of wholeness rather than a reaction to lack.

This process is neither linear nor instantaneous. Identity change involves setbacks, doubts, and old patterns resurfacing under stress. But each decision aligned with your new narrative—each moment of courage, each small financial win, each act of conscious choice—reinforces the new architecture. Over time, what once felt aspirational becomes integrated. You are no longer performing wealth—you are inhabiting it.

To rewrite your wealth identity is to declare sovereignty over your financial story. It is to shift from inherited scripts to intentional authorship. It is not about how much you have, but about how clearly and courageously you claim your capacity to have, to hold, and to grow. When that claim is made—not with arrogance but with awareness—you step into a new role: not the struggling character in someone else's script, but the conscious creator of a life defined by alignment, agency, and abundance. And from that place, wealth becomes not just possible, but inevitable.

Chapter 3
Limiting Beliefs and the Money Mind Recode

Most people assume financial difficulties stem from figures—deficits, debts, or a lack of savings. But look closer, and you'll often find the real trouble begins much earlier, in the quiet formation of narratives. Not budgeting errors, but internal scripts. "I'm not good with money." "Wealth isn't for people like me." "It's too late now." These phrases, repeated often enough, slide into the mind like background music—unquestioned, oddly persuasive. They masquerade as facts or self-awareness, when in truth, they're nothing more than unexamined beliefs. And those beliefs—so familiar we hardly notice them—build the invisible walls that keep us circling within the same financial patterns, no matter how hard we try to change.

This chapter is a map of those mental boundaries—and a guide to taking them apart. At its heart lies a simple but powerful idea: our beliefs about money are not set in stone. They're not innate, and they're certainly not immune to change. Like habits, they're learned—acquired through repetition, emotional charge, and reinforcement over time. And, crucially, they can be unlearned. To reimagine your financial life, you must first interrogate the mental software quietly driving it. This isn't a call for shallow positivity or cheerleading slogans about abundance. It's a disciplined reconditioning of the mind, informed by neuroscience, psychology, and behaviour design. The goal? To build a belief system that aligns with your aspirations, rather than undermining them.

Understanding how beliefs are formed—and how they embed themselves—is critical. A belief is not just an idea. It's a neurological groove, a well-worn pathway in the brain. The mind, always keen to conserve energy, clings to familiar scripts. So when you hear, again and again, that "money is stressful" or "wealthy people are greedy," your brain doesn't debate the statement—it stores it, files it away, and starts filtering new experiences through its lens. Familiarity becomes mistaken for truth.

Thankfully, that same machinery—the brain's efficiency-seeking autopilot—also makes it possible to change course. Thanks to neuroplasticity, we now understand that the brain can rewire itself, even in adulthood. Beliefs, once embedded, are not beyond reach. They can be interrupted, interrogated, and rewritten. Of course, it's not instantaneous. But with consistency, the mental grooves of scarcity, fear, or resignation can be reshaped into something more useful—something that opens doors instead of closing them.

The trouble is, limiting beliefs often don't look like limitations. They show up cloaked in common sense, wrapped in social norms. Consider the statement, "I just want to be comfortable." Sounds fair enough, doesn't it? But for some, it's a mask—one that hides a fear of visibility, or a deeper discomfort with success and all the responsibility it brings. Or take "I'm too old to start investing." It feels like a logical conclusion, but often it's a protective mechanism—shielding one from the risk of disappointment, the pain of regret. These sorts of beliefs don't shout; they whisper. And detecting them requires more than self-awareness—it requires unflinching honesty.

Take James, for example—a 52-year-old architect who had never once invested beyond his pension. When asked why, he shrugged: "I missed the boat. Starting in my thirties would've made sense, but now? It's pointless." This belief had hardened over time, providing a neat excuse to avoid the discomfort of learning something new. But when he finally paused to scrutinise it—with the help of a financial adviser—he discovered something quite different. The numbers, once run, showed that he still had time to grow his wealth meaningfully. It wasn't the years that were the issue; it was the belief that had ossified into identity.

Beliefs don't just sit idle in the mind—they loop into behaviour, reinforcing themselves with every repetition. If you believe you're "bad with money," you may avoid looking at your bank account. That leads to missed bills, mounting stress, and eventually, more evidence to support your belief. It becomes self-fulfilling. And the longer the loop runs, the more difficult it becomes to imagine any alternative. To interrupt that cycle, you need to disrupt both thought and action—each reinforcing the other.

This is where belief flipping comes into play. It's not about smothering a negative thought with forced optimism. It's about exposing the belief to the light, tracing its roots, and then deliberately replacing it with something more empowering—but crucially, something you can believe. Declaring "I'm great with money now" might ring hollow. But "I'm learning to build financial systems that fit who I am" feels grounded. It acknowledges past struggles without being defined by them. And it opens a door forward.

To embed this shift, a simple framework—anchor, affirmation, action—can prove surprisingly effective. The anchor is your new core belief, the foundation upon which you want to build. The affirmation is the language you use to reinforce it—spoken, written, or simply repeated in thought. The action is what brings it to life. Not grand gestures—just small, consistent steps that reinforce the new narrative. Belief without behaviour becomes abstraction. Behaviour without belief lacks staying power. But together, they reinforce the change.

Imagine someone trying to escape scarcity thinking. They might choose as their anchor: "There is enough, and I am capable of creating more." Their affirmation? "I trust myself to grow and manage my wealth." And their action? A weekly check-in with their finances, not as a chore, but as an act of curiosity and self-respect. Repeating this triad over time gradually rewires not just thoughts, but emotional associations—transforming money from a source of anxiety into one of agency.

Still, no one lives in a vacuum. Often, the beliefs we carry aren't just personal—they're generational, even cultural. Messages like "We're not the kind of people who get rich," or "Money changes people," or "Be careful—money ruins families" have long roots. They might have served a purpose once, in a context of real hardship or marginalisation. But today, those inherited narratives can become chains. Rewriting your financial story may mean grieving the old script. Not with disdain, but with gratitude—and the understanding that a new context demands a new mindset.

At its core, this work is about reclaiming authorship. You are no longer a passive recipient of belief, shaped by accident or inheritance.

You become an active participant, shaping your inner landscape with intention. It's not easy. There will be backslides, moments of doubt, perhaps even shame. But these are not indicators of failure—they are proof that rewiring is underway.

What this chapter offers is more than theory. It lays out tools and perspectives designed to move belief from the abstract to the actionable. Because true financial change isn't just about spreadsheets or strategies—it's about shifting the identity that drives them. It's about becoming someone who believes they can earn well, spend wisely, invest with confidence, and hold abundance without flinching.

Your financial mindset isn't fixed. It bends, evolves, transforms—if you let it. And in that transformation lies the possibility of an entirely new reality. One where your choices are guided not by inherited fears, but by clarity, ownership, and a growing trust in who you are becoming.

Spotting Limiting Beliefs in Disguise

When it comes to money, most of us believe we're making decisions based on reason, facts, and practicalities. Yet beneath those surface-level justifications often lie deeply embedded beliefs—beliefs that shape our financial behaviours in ways we rarely recognise. These beliefs are not always loud or obviously destructive. More often, they are quiet, familiar, and seemingly rational. But their true power lies in their stealth: they operate beneath our conscious awareness, guiding decisions, creating inertia, and reinforcing a financial status quo that no longer serves us.

Limiting beliefs are internalised convictions that set boundaries on what we believe is possible, permissible, or appropriate for us. In the context of money, they act like a mental governor on a car—no matter how powerful the engine or how clear the road ahead, we won't go faster than what the internal programming allows. These beliefs don't always arrive with fanfare. They whisper in the background, often in the language of logic or self-protection. Statements like "I'm bad with money," "It's too late to start saving," or "Money changes people" are not neutral observations; they are disguised limitations masquerading as common sense.

Take, for instance, the phrase *"I'm just not a numbers person."* It's an innocuous remark, often delivered with a self-deprecating chuckle. But embedded in that sentiment is a belief that financial literacy is innate rather than learnable, and that money management is reserved for a certain kind of mind. This belief creates a barrier to financial education, discouraging the very behaviours—curiosity, learning, engagement—that would dismantle the barrier itself. The person holding this belief may outsource decisions blindly, avoid financial planning altogether, or become chronically dependent on others, perpetuating a cycle of disempowerment.

Similarly, *"It's too late for me"* is a particularly insidious belief, cloaked in the language of realism. It's the phrase many use to justify inaction in middle age or beyond, convincing themselves that missed opportunities in their twenties or thirties have rendered future progress pointless. But the belief conflates time lost with time wasted. The reality is that financial growth is rarely linear and is almost always recoverable. Compounded progress—whether through investing, income expansion, or debt reduction—can happen at any age, provided the underlying belief in possibility is intact. The danger of "too late" thinking is that it not only limits action but erodes hope, reducing the emotional fuel needed to drive change.

Another widespread belief is *"Money changes people."* Often stated as a truism, this phrase carries a tone of moral caution—as though wealth inevitably corrupts character or severs community ties. While it is true that money amplifies one's choices and can alter social dynamics, the belief itself is frequently used to self-sabotage or to pre-emptively distance oneself from abundance. Those who hold this belief may resist asking for a raise, undercharge for their services, or avoid investing—even when it is clearly in their best interest—out of fear that financial success will alienate them from their values or communities. In this way, a belief that appears to be about others is really a protective strategy for avoiding discomfort around personal growth.

To identify these disguised beliefs, we must adopt the mindset of an internal detective. One effective method is to track the language you use when thinking or speaking about money. Phrases that begin with "I always," "I never," "People like me," or "That's just how it is" often signal the presence of a fixed belief. These statements are rarely factual. They are emotionally anchored conclusions drawn from past experiences, social conditioning, or cultural messaging. Yet once they take root, they act as filters—distorting how we interpret new information and constraining our perceived options.

Consider the case of Amina, a second-generation immigrant and successful entrepreneur who, despite growing revenues in her business, found herself resisting reinvestment and growth. She repeatedly told herself, "It could all disappear tomorrow." On the surface, this sounded like prudence. But under examination, it became clear that this belief stemmed from her parents' lived experience of economic volatility and displacement. Her inherited caution, while valid in its historical context, was now obstructing her capacity to scale. When she acknowledged the origin of the belief, she was able to separate inherited fear from present-day reality. She began to build a financial buffer that honoured her family's history while taking measured steps towards expansion.

Limiting beliefs also manifest in interpersonal dynamics. For example, *"I'll be judged if I talk about money"* can inhibit essential conversations between partners, colleagues, or friends. This belief, rooted in social taboos, keeps financial life siloed and shame-driven. It discourages collaboration, perpetuates ignorance, and allows misinformation to flourish. The belief is often justified by past experiences—dismissive responses, embarrassment, or cultural norms—but when internalised, it becomes a script that cuts us off from vital resources: knowledge, support, and accountability.

To disrupt these internal scripts, it is important to not only spot them but to question their validity and relevance. Begin by asking: *Is this belief objectively true, or is it familiar? When did I first learn it? Whose voice does it echo? What is it protecting me from? And what would become possible if I no longer believed it?* These questions don't demand immediate answers—they invite reflection. And that reflection creates cognitive space for alternative narratives to emerge.

Take Jordan, a graphic designer in his early forties who consistently avoided setting financial goals. When asked why, he said, "If I make a plan, I'll just fail at it." At first glance, this seemed like an issue of motivation. But deeper exploration revealed a pattern of perfectionism rooted in childhood experiences of harsh criticism. Avoiding financial planning wasn't laziness—it was self-protection. By believing that failure was inevitable, Jordan spared himself the pain of falling short. Yet he also denied himself the satisfaction of progress. Once he identified this belief, he was able to experiment with low-stakes planning and celebrate small wins, gradually building the confidence that allowed a new identity to take shape.

It's important to emphasise that limiting beliefs are not irrational. They often have a protective function. They help us avoid discomfort, conflict, risk, or emotional vulnerability. But the protection they offer is usually outdated. A belief formed to shield us from scarcity or shame in the past may now be holding us back from freedom and expansion. Releasing these beliefs does not mean invalidating past pain—it means choosing not to let it dictate future possibility.

The process of spotting and reshaping limiting beliefs is not a one-time event. It is an ongoing practice, much like physical conditioning or skill-building. The brain is wired to seek familiarity, and old beliefs will resurface under stress, uncertainty, or transition. But each time we meet them with awareness rather than autopilot, we weaken their grip. We replace rigidity with flexibility, fear with discernment, limitation with choice.

Ultimately, the beliefs that shape your financial life are not simply reflections of reality—they are authors of it. If you believe that money is hard to earn, you will likely resist opportunities that come easily. If you believe you are not "the type" to be wealthy, you will find subtle ways to remain underpaid or financially insecure. But if you learn to identify and challenge these beliefs, to hold them up to the light and examine their origins, you create the space to choose differently. And in that space, the architecture of your financial future begins to change—brick by brick, belief by belief.

Spotting limiting beliefs in disguise is an act of both humility and courage. It requires us to admit that our internal compass may need recalibration—and that our reality is, in many ways, a mirror of our mindset. But it also reminds us that beliefs are not facts. They are choices. And once you see them clearly, you can begin to write new ones—ones that honour your past, reflect your present, and support the future you are ready to create.

The Science of Belief Formation

The human brain is a pattern-detecting, meaning-making organ, exquisitely designed to turn experience into expectation and observation into belief. When it comes to money, however, this elegant system often becomes a double-edged sword. Our financial behaviours—how we earn, save, invest, or avoid money—are not merely the result of logical thinking or strategic planning. They are deeply influenced by neurological imprints: learned associations and belief structures that have been reinforced over years, often decades. To shift these patterns meaningfully, we must first understand how they are formed, how they operate, and—crucially—how they can be rewired.

Belief formation, at its core, is a neurological process shaped by exposure, repetition, emotion, and reinforcement. From infancy, the brain begins encoding responses to environmental stimuli. If money is discussed with anxiety or secrecy in a household, a child may begin to associate financial matters with tension or shame. If spending is used to soothe emotional distress, a belief may form that purchases equal comfort or self-worth. These associations are not conscious choices; they are the brain's way of creating heuristics—shortcuts that allow us to process complex information quickly and act efficiently in everyday life.

At the centre of this process lies the brain's limbic system, particularly the amygdala and hippocampus, which are responsible for emotional memory and threat detection. Emotional experiences—especially those linked to survival, fear, or social belonging—are prioritised in the brain's architecture. This means that emotionally charged financial experiences, such as witnessing a parent lose a job or experiencing a period of intense scarcity, leave a disproportionate imprint. The more emotionally vivid the event, the more firmly it becomes encoded in our neural pathways.

Take the example of Samira, a successful lawyer who, despite earning a six-figure income, struggled with persistent anxiety around spending. Even small purchases triggered feelings of guilt and unease. Through financial therapy, she uncovered that her father had once lost his business due to risky investments, leading to a prolonged period of economic hardship during her adolescence. The memory of that instability had shaped a powerful belief: that spending money was inherently dangerous. Her brain had wired this association not because it was objectively true in all cases, but because it had been emotionally relevant in a critical developmental window.

Neuroscience tells us that the brain's default mode is to conserve energy, and it does so by reinforcing familiar patterns. When a belief is formed, particularly in the context of emotion or repetition, it creates a neural pathway—a connection between neurons that is strengthened each time the belief is activated. The more frequently a person thinks *"I'm bad with money"* or avoids checking their account, the more entrenched that belief becomes. Over time, the brain stops questioning the belief's validity. It simply uses the well-worn path, even if it leads to dysfunctional or limiting behaviour.

The good news is that the brain is not static. Thanks to the principle of neuroplasticity, it is possible to change these patterns. Neuroplasticity refers to the brain's ability to reorganise itself by forming new neural connections throughout life. This capacity means that old, unhelpful beliefs can be challenged and replaced with new ones—provided they are repeated consistently, emotionally reinforced, and supported by behaviour.

But belief rewiring is not a process of brute force or denial. Simply replacing *"I'm bad with money"* with *"I'm great with money"* can create cognitive dissonance if it does not feel believable. The brain resists statements that contradict its current programming unless they are scaffolded by incremental proof. This is where the integration of behavioural micro-steps, cognitive reframing, and emotional regulation becomes essential.

For example, cognitive behavioural therapy (CBT), which has been widely studied for its efficacy in modifying thought patterns, focuses on identifying automatic thoughts, questioning their validity, and replacing them with more balanced alternatives. In financial terms, a person who routinely thinks *"I'll never get out of debt"* would learn to identify that belief, challenge the evidence behind it, and experiment with more accurate narratives like *"My debt is real, but I have options and resources I can build on."* Over time, as these new thoughts are repeated and supported by small wins—such as paying down a credit card or setting up a budget—they begin to form new neural pathways, eventually becoming the brain's new default.

The somatic dimension of belief formation also warrants attention. Our bodies play a critical role in encoding and recalling belief-laden experiences. Financial fear, for example, often manifests physiologically: tightness in the chest when logging into a bank account, a spike in heart rate during a money conversation, or tension headaches after reviewing bills. These bodily responses are not just stress—they are learned associations between money and threat. To rewire belief at a deep level, it's important to include practices that engage the body's stress response and signal safety.

Mindfulness, breathwork, and other regulation techniques help calm the nervous system, making it easier for the brain to adopt new beliefs. When the body feels safe, the brain becomes more plastic—more receptive to change. This is one reason why belief shifts tend to happen not in moments of pressure or panic, but in calm, reflective states. A regular practice of financial reflection—perhaps through journaling, meditation, or quiet review—can help integrate new beliefs more effectively than sporadic, crisis-driven efforts.

The environment also plays a critical role in reinforcing or challenging our financial beliefs. We do not form our money mindsets in isolation; they are shaped by families, peers, media, and cultural narratives. If you grew up hearing "rich people are greedy" or "money doesn't grow on trees," those phrases may have embedded themselves into your subconscious not because of their accuracy, but because of their repetition and the authority of the voices delivering them. In adulthood, surrounding oneself with people who model healthy, empowered financial behaviours can serve as a powerful counterweight to those early influences.

Consider Marcus, a teacher in his late thirties who believed that financial abundance was inherently selfish. Raised in a working-class household where financial struggle was normalised and frugality was a moral value, he equated wealth with social detachment. It wasn't until he joined a professional network of educators focused on financial empowerment that he began to see alternative models—people who earned well, gave generously, and remained deeply connected to their communities. This exposure provided a new narrative, offering his brain the social proof it needed to question and ultimately reshape its belief.

It's important to recognise that not all beliefs are negative simply because they are old. Some inherited beliefs may still serve us—such as valuing saving, avoiding unnecessary debt, or giving back to others. The key is not to reject all past programming, but to sift through it consciously. Ask: *Does this belief support the person I am becoming? Is it grounded in truth or fear? Do I choose it freely or out of habit?*

Rewriting your financial beliefs is a process of both excavation and authorship. It requires digging into the neural and emotional origins of your current money mindset and making deliberate choices about which beliefs to keep, which to question, and which to replace. It is a dynamic interplay between neuroscience and narrative—between the plasticity of your brain and the power of your personal story.

This chapter invites you not only to understand belief formation intellectually but to engage with it experientially. By bringing curiosity to your financial behaviours, attentiveness to your inner dialogue, and patience to the process of change, you can begin to recode your mind for a different financial future. Not one driven by outdated scripts, inherited fear, or reactive habits, but by a conscious, empowered belief system that reflects your highest aspirations and values.

Beliefs are not destiny. They are habits of thought—formed, reinforced, and entirely within your capacity to transform. With clarity, intention, and repetition, you can reshape the architecture of your financial mind—and from that foundation, build a wealth experience defined not by default, but by design.

Challenging the Belief–Behaviour Feedback Loop

The financial lives we lead are shaped less by what we know and more by what we believe. These beliefs, often unconscious and inherited, are not inert. They are active agents in a self-reinforcing system—one where belief shapes behaviour, behaviour generates outcomes, and outcomes validate the original belief. This closed loop, known in psychological and behavioural economics circles as the *belief–behaviour feedback loop*, is one of the most powerful forces driving financial decision-making. Understanding and disrupting this cycle is not only central to financial transformation—it is fundamental to reclaiming personal agency in all areas of life.

At its core, the belief–behaviour feedback loop begins with a mental script, a lens through which the brain interprets financial information. If that lens is one of scarcity—*"I'll never have enough"*—then every financial action is filtered through that expectation. A person who holds this belief may avoid budgeting because it feels futile, refuse to ask for a raise because it seems pointless, or impulsively spend out of the assumption that any money will disappear anyway. When these behaviours inevitably produce results that fall short—bills unpaid, savings depleted, opportunities missed—they reinforce the initial belief. The outcome becomes proof that the original assumption was correct.

This pattern is deeply entrenched in human cognition. The brain is constantly seeking coherence between what it believes and what it experiences. This tendency, known as *confirmation bias*, leads us to selectively attend to information that supports our existing views while ignoring or downplaying contradictory evidence. For instance, someone who believes they are "bad with money" will focus on every misstep—a forgotten subscription, a declined card, a late payment—while discounting their successes, such as negotiating a discount, paying off a debt, or sticking to a budget for several weeks. The loop closes, reinforcing not reality, but perception.

Real-world examples bring this to life with striking clarity. Take Laura, a mid-level manager in her forties who had internalised the belief that she "just wasn't financially savvy." This belief, inherited from growing up in a household where money was a source of constant stress, had calcified into identity. Despite earning a stable income, Laura avoided looking at her bank statements, refused to engage with her retirement planning, and relied on her partner to make all financial decisions. Each act of avoidance affirmed her sense of inadequacy, and the resulting disorganisation in her finances reinforced her initial narrative. The belief and the behaviour were locked in mutual reinforcement.

To challenge this loop, one must first interrupt it. And interruption begins with *awareness*. This means identifying the underlying belief that is driving the behaviour. Often, these beliefs are not obvious. They hide behind excuses, rationalisations, or vague discomfort. "I'm too busy to budget" might mask a deeper fear of confronting past mistakes. "I don't care about money" could conceal anxiety about inadequacy or fear of change. The task is to name the belief clearly, without judgment, and to trace its origins. Where did this belief come from? Whose voice does it echo? What assumptions is it built on?

Once the belief is identified, the next step is to test its validity—not abstractly, but behaviourally. This is where change must move from cognition to action. Because the belief–behaviour loop is sustained by repeated experiences, the only way to dismantle it is to create *new* experiences that generate *new* evidence. This is not about massive shifts or sweeping declarations. It is about small, strategic actions that challenge the belief at its foundation.

Consider Daniel, a freelance photographer who believed he was "not the kind of person who invests." This belief, shaped by a family culture of financial caution and reinforced by a lack of formal education, had kept him from engaging with any form of long-term planning. Rather than attempting to become an overnight investment expert, Daniel started by reading one article a week, then opened a modest investment account with automatic contributions. As he gained familiarity, his discomfort began to diminish. Over time, his behaviour shifted, and with it, so did his belief. He no longer saw investing as something reserved for others, but as a normal and accessible part of his financial life.

Crucially, what Daniel did was create *disconfirming evidence*—experiences that contradicted his existing belief and offered the brain a new narrative to consider. Neuroscience tells us that the brain's default is to preserve the status quo. But when faced with repeated, emotionally neutral or positive evidence that a belief is no longer valid, it begins to rewire. This is the foundation of neuroplasticity, and it is particularly powerful when paired with reflective practices such as journaling, coaching, or therapy, which allow the individual to articulate and reinforce the shift.

However, disruption alone is not sufficient. For the new behaviour to stick, it must be reinforced consistently. This is where intentional habit design becomes essential. The more frequently a new behaviour is performed, especially in moments of low resistance, the more deeply it becomes embedded in the brain's reward system. For example, someone trying to break the belief *"I'm terrible with money"* might set a weekly ritual of reviewing their finances in a calm, structured way—perhaps with music, tea, or a sense of ritual. Over time, this recontextualises financial engagement as manageable and even pleasant, countering the emotional associations that once underpinned avoidance.

But the loop also requires a shift in *identity language*. The words we use to describe ourselves reinforce the beliefs we hold. Saying "I'm trying to get better with money" keeps the individual in a state of conditional change—where success is always deferred. In contrast, stating "I'm someone who is learning to handle money well" acknowledges progress and reinforces a growth identity. This subtle shift has powerful implications. Language shapes cognition, and cognition shapes action.

The belief–behaviour loop is not merely psychological; it is deeply physiological. The stress response, activated by fear or uncertainty, can shut down executive function in the brain, impairing planning, decision-making, and emotional regulation. When financial decisions are made from a place of fear—triggered by beliefs of inadequacy or scarcity—the prefrontal cortex is less active, and the amygdala takes over. This results in reactive, short-term thinking. To break this pattern, practices that regulate the nervous system—such as breathwork, meditation, or physical movement—are not just wellness add-ons; they are integral to rewiring the belief–behaviour cycle.

It is also important to contextualise the loop within broader systems of culture, inequality, and access. Many beliefs about money are not merely personal—they are shaped by socioeconomic background, racial and gender dynamics, and historical traumas. A woman who believes it is inappropriate to negotiate her salary may be responding not to internal inadequacy, but to repeated social penalties for assertiveness. A person of colour who hesitates to invest may carry intergenerational memories of exclusion from wealth-building opportunities. Challenging these beliefs, therefore, is not only a personal act—it is a political and cultural one. It requires both individual agency and systemic awareness.

Challenging the belief–behaviour feedback loop is an act of conscious leadership over one's life. It demands rigour and self-compassion in equal measure. There will be setbacks—moments when the old belief resurfaces, triggered by stress, failure, or external judgment. But these are not signs of regression. They are invitations to reaffirm the new belief, to return to the new behaviour, and to continue the cycle of evidence, reinforcement, and growth.

Ultimately, the loop is neither enemy nor destiny. It is a system—one that, once understood, can be rewired. With every conscious action taken against a limiting belief, you create a new neural imprint. With every repetition, you strengthen it. And with enough repetition, the new belief becomes the new default—not through force, but through familiarity. This is the quiet revolution of financial transformation. It is not flashy. It is not overnight. But it is profound, durable, and entirely within reach.

The question is no longer *what do you believe?* The question is *what are you repeatedly doing to prove it?* And if the answer does not serve you—then it is time to change the loop.

Belief Flipping: From Scarcity to Strategy

The most persistent obstacles to financial growth are rarely found in the economy, interest rates, or spreadsheets. They are internal, rooted in the scripts we absorb and replay throughout our lives—scripts that whisper what is "realistic," what is "deserved," or what is "safe." These internalised narratives, commonly referred to as limiting beliefs, shape not only how we think about money but how we behave with it. Left unchallenged, they form the mental scaffolding of a scarcity mindset—an orientation that sees lack rather than potential, risk rather than opportunity, and shame rather than agency. Belief flipping is the deliberate, structured act of confronting these inherited narratives and converting them into strategies that serve our current goals, values, and capacities.

Beliefs are not objective truths. They are interpretations—cognitive shortcuts reinforced through repetition, emotion, and past experience. When a belief like *"I'm just bad with money"* goes unexamined, it begins to function as identity. It informs how a person navigates financial choices, often triggering avoidance, procrastination, or disempowerment. The longer it remains in place, the more evidence the mind collects to support it, strengthening the neural pathways that carry the belief. This is where belief flipping becomes a powerful psychological and behavioural intervention. It disrupts the automatic loop and replaces it with intentional thought patterns, backed by emotional logic and practical evidence.

To flip a belief from scarcity to strategy, we must begin by identifying it with precision. The first step is to listen carefully to our internal dialogue, especially in moments of financial discomfort—during budget reviews, investment decisions, or pricing conversations. Common limiting beliefs often sound deceptively benign: *"I don't care about money," "People like me don't get rich," "We're just not a money family,"* or *"I'll deal with this later."* These phrases do not simply describe reality; they *create* it. They are protective mechanisms, often designed to shield us from fear, failure, or social discomfort, but they do so at the cost of progress.

Consider the case of Elena, a first-generation entrepreneur who consistently undercharged for her consulting services. Her internal belief—*"If I ask for more, I'll lose the client"*—was shaped by early memories of watching her parents negotiate every household expense with trepidation. Money, for her, was always precarious, and financial assertiveness felt emotionally dangerous. But when she paused to examine the belief, she realised it was not only untested but outdated. Through deliberate reflection, she reframed it: *"The right clients will value my work when I communicate my value clearly."* She supported this new belief with logical evidence—client testimonials, results she had delivered, and industry benchmarks. As she began charging aligned rates, not only did she retain more clients than she feared, but her self-concept also evolved to match her new actions.

What made Elena's shift effective was not just positive thinking, but structured affirmation grounded in evidence. This is where belief flipping distinguishes itself from vague motivational platitudes. It does not ask you to deny your past or fake certainty. Instead, it invites you to meet your limiting belief with logic, compassion, and a reframe that aligns with your present goals.

To engage in this process yourself, start by isolating a specific belief that frequently surfaces in your financial life. Write it down verbatim, without editing. Next, ask: *Is this belief universally true? When did I first hear it? Who taught it to me—directly or indirectly? What emotional payoff does it offer (protection, avoidance, belonging)? What does it cost me to keep it?*

Now, construct a new belief—a statement that maintains emotional resonance but shifts the orientation from helplessness to strategy. This reframe should not simply oppose the old belief, but offer a grounded alternative. For instance:

Old belief: *"I'll never have enough."*
Reframed belief: *"I am learning to manage and grow what I have, and I am building capacity for more."*

Old belief: *"I don't deserve wealth."*
Reframed belief: *"I am learning that my worth is not dependent on past messages, and I have the right to financial stability and joy."*

Old belief: *"Money always creates conflict."*
Reframed belief: *"With clear communication and healthy boundaries, money can strengthen relationships and support shared values."*

Each new belief gains strength when supported by real-life evidence. Look for examples in your own history where you succeeded financially, made a wise decision, or advocated for yourself. If such evidence feels scarce, borrow from others. Read case studies, talk to mentors, or study peers who have made the shift you aspire to. The brain does not require *personal* evidence to begin reprogramming—it requires *credible* evidence, repeated with consistency and paired with positive emotion.

The final—and perhaps most crucial—component of belief flipping is behavioural integration. A new belief cannot take root without new behaviour. If you adopt the belief *"I can handle my finances,"* but continue to avoid reviewing your accounts, the brain will default to its old wiring. But if you begin to act in alignment with your new narrative, even in small ways—tracking expenses weekly, asking a question in a financial webinar, or automating savings—the behaviour begins to reinforce the belief. Over time, this repetition strengthens the neural pathway until it becomes the new default.

Marcus, a 29-year-old musician, struggled with the belief that financial planning was incompatible with his creative identity. The implicit narrative was *"Artists aren't supposed to care about money—it's selling out."* This belief led him to avoid setting financial goals or creating systems, which in turn caused frequent stress and reactive decisions. When he worked to reframe this belief, he landed on: *"Caring about money gives me the freedom to create without fear."* To reinforce this, he began a weekly "financial studio session," treating money management as a creative act. Within a year, Marcus had stabilised his income, paid off significant debt, and released a new album on his own terms. His creativity didn't shrink with financial clarity—it expanded.

These transformations are not unique. Across sectors—from small business owners to corporate professionals, from students to retirees—the practice of belief flipping is quietly reshaping the way people approach wealth, not as a battleground of morality or luck, but as a domain of strategy, agency, and possibility.

It is worth noting that belief flipping is not about relentless positivity or denying the reality of structural barriers. Economic inequality, financial trauma, and systemic bias are real. But even within these constraints, the beliefs we hold about what is possible, what is deserved, and what is safe remain among the most powerful levers of personal change. Belief flipping is not a cure-all, but it is a catalyst—a method for reclaiming authorship over one's internal narrative and using that authorship to create external change.

As with all meaningful transformation, this process requires time, patience, and repetition. Old beliefs may resurface under stress or uncertainty, and that is natural. But each time you meet them with your new narrative—each time you choose strategy over scarcity—you reinforce your new identity. You teach your brain, through action and affirmation, that a different way is not only possible but already unfolding.

Ultimately, belief flipping is not just about money. It is about the kind of relationship you want to have with yourself—one grounded in self-trust, vision, and clarity. The scarcity mindset says, "This is all there is, so protect it, fear it, or deny it." A strategic mindset says, "Let's understand where we are, and let's build something better—with intelligence, intention, and heart." That shift begins with one thought, one reframe, one action—and the willingness to believe that change is not only deserved, but already within reach.

Building the New Belief System

Transforming your financial reality begins not with tactics, but with an inner reconfiguration. While spreadsheets and strategies certainly matter, they are only as effective as the beliefs that drive them. Most individuals who struggle with money are not failing because they lack discipline or intelligence, but because their internal operating system—the set of beliefs, assumptions, and emotional associations they hold around money—has not been updated to support the goals they aspire to. Belief precedes behaviour. And when belief is rooted in scarcity, inadequacy, or fear, even the most logical financial plans can unravel. To initiate sustainable change, we must learn how to build a belief system that is congruent with financial confidence, clarity, and self-trust.

The process of building a new belief system is not abstract wishful thinking. It is an applied psychological practice, grounded in research on neuroplasticity, behavioural conditioning, and identity transformation. It begins with a simple but powerful three-part framework: anchor, affirmation, and action. These three components work in unison to replace limiting beliefs with empowered ones, reinforcing new neural pathways through conscious thought, embodied language, and behaviour-based reinforcement.

The first step is to establish an *anchor*. An anchor is a core belief that reflects your desired financial identity. Unlike a goal—which is specific and measurable—an anchor is a principle that guides how you see yourself in relation to money. It is the emotional and cognitive foundation upon which your new behaviours are built. For instance, someone shifting from a scarcity-based mindset might choose an anchor like *"I am capable of building and sustaining wealth,"* or *"I trust myself to make sound financial decisions."* The anchor must feel authentic, not performative. It should stretch your current self-concept, but not contradict it so severely that your mind rejects it.

Anchors work best when they address not only behaviour, but identity. Research in behavioural science has consistently shown that identity-based change is more durable than outcome-based change. A person who sees themselves as "the kind of person who saves regularly" is more likely to sustain saving habits than someone merely focused on hitting a number. Anchors help shift internal identity so that external behaviour becomes an expression of who you are, not just something you are trying to do.

Next comes the *affirmation*—the language you use to internalise and reinforce your anchor. This is not the hollow, cheerleading-style self-talk that popular culture often associates with affirmations. Effective affirmations are carefully chosen, linguistically precise, and emotionally grounded. They reflect the reality you are stepping into, rather than denying the one you are leaving. For example, rather than repeating *"I'm rich and successful"* when you feel insecure about money, a more effective affirmation might be *"I am developing the skills and mindset that support long-term financial stability."* The goal is to speak in a way that bridges the gap between your current state and your desired state—affirming progress without pretending certainty.

Affirmations also play a neurological role. When spoken aloud, written down, or even mentally rehearsed with emotional engagement, they activate areas of the brain associated with self-referential thinking and emotional regulation. Over time, repeated affirmations begin to weaken the synaptic strength of the old belief and replace it with a new pattern. This is neuroplasticity in action—the brain's ability to rewire itself based on experience and repetition.

But no belief system is complete without the third and most crucial component: *action.* Action is the behaviour that reinforces your anchor and gives your affirmation real-world evidence. Without action, even the most inspiring internal narratives remain hypothetical. Behavioural change validates the new belief and teaches the brain that this new way of thinking is not only possible—it's safe and effective.

Consider Rahul, a software engineer who had long carried the belief that he was "terrible with money." This belief, seeded during a chaotic financial period in university, persisted into his adult life, despite a steady income and growing career. His anchor became: *"I am learning to lead my financial life with calm and clarity."* His affirmation was: *"Every small step I take brings me closer to financial confidence."* To reinforce this, he took the action of setting a weekly financial check-in on Sunday afternoons. He used that time to review transactions, set intentions for the week, and update a simple progress tracker. Over six months, Rahul not only paid down credit card debt but began investing regularly. More importantly, his internal narrative shifted—from self-doubt to self-respect.

What made Rahul's transformation sustainable was the integration of these three elements. His anchor gave him a sense of direction. His affirmation gave him emotional language to carry into moments of resistance. And his consistent action created the feedback loop that rewired his belief system.

Another example is Lydia, a creative freelancer who historically saw budgeting as restrictive and emotionally draining. Her old belief was *"Money limits my freedom."* After reflecting on the impact of that narrative—sporadic saving, reactive spending, and periodic anxiety—she decided to flip it. Her new anchor was: *"Financial structure amplifies my freedom."* Her affirmation became: *"Budgeting helps me express my values, not restrict them."* She began allocating a monthly budget not just for necessities, but for joy—books, travel, creative tools—redefining money management as self-expression. This reframing led her to approach finances with enthusiasm, not dread, and to see wealth as a canvas, not a cage.

Such examples underscore that building a new belief system is not about pretending difficulties don't exist. It is about shifting from a default mode of fear or avoidance to a proactive stance rooted in trust, values, and strategy. Anchors help ground the shift. Affirmations reprogram the internal dialogue. Actions provide the proof the mind needs to update its expectations.

Importantly, this framework allows for personalisation. Each person's anchors, affirmations, and actions will be unique, shaped by their values, personality, and context. There is no one-size-fits-all formula. What matters is coherence—the degree to which your inner narrative and outer behaviour are aligned. When you say you believe in abundance, but act from fear, the cognitive dissonance will eventually erode both belief and momentum. But when belief and action are in sync, change becomes not only possible, but sustainable.

This process also builds psychological resilience. In financial life, setbacks are inevitable—an unexpected expense, a market downturn, a lost client. A strong belief system does not prevent adversity, but it buffers its impact. Anchored beliefs, reinforced through consistent action, give you a stable centre from which to respond rather than react. They allow you to see setbacks as feedback, not failure.

Moreover, this work extends beyond money. As your belief system shifts, you may notice changes in how you approach time, relationships, creativity, and risk. A person who believes *"I am worthy of growth and support"* will not only manage their finances differently—they will seek better jobs, negotiate more confidently, and set healthier boundaries. Financial transformation, then, becomes a portal to a broader personal evolution.

Building a new belief system is not a one-off exercise. It is a dynamic, iterative process that evolves with you. Anchors may need to be revisited. Affirmations may deepen or become more specific. Actions may shift as your context changes. But with intentionality and consistency, this triad—anchor, affirmation, and action—becomes the foundation of a more empowered, strategic, and self-aligned financial identity.

Beliefs are not immutable truths. They are stories we tell ourselves, shaped by the past but open to revision. When we take responsibility for those stories—by anchoring them in values, articulating them with care, and backing them with aligned action—we do more than improve our finances. We reclaim authorship of our lives. And from that place, money becomes not a source of shame or confusion, but a tool for clarity, integrity, and lasting fulfilment.

Chapter 4
Emotional Spending, Guilt Saving, and the Financial Nervous System

Money, when you strip away the spreadsheets and statements, is rarely just about numbers. Beneath the surface of nearly every financial decision pulses an emotional undercurrent—a subtle, often unconscious negotiation between reason and something far older: our nervous systems, our formative experiences, the coping habits we've quietly collected over time. Whether it's tapping "buy now" after a hard day, shelving an investment opportunity because it stirs up unease, or feeling a faint stab of guilt over a well-earned treat, the real terrain we're navigating isn't fiscal. It's physiological. Psychological. This chapter delves into that seldom-charted intersection between emotional regulation and financial behaviour—an axis as potent as it is under-acknowledged in the way we relate to money today.

To grasp how emotion shapes our financial choices, we first need to reframe money itself—not as mere currency, but as a stand-in for unmet needs. Emotional spending, contrary to what moralising headlines might suggest, isn't just frivolity. More often, it's an attempt to self-soothe. A salve for stress. A bid for control. A quiet plea for recognition or relief. Think of it this way: just as food, alcohol, or digital distractions can serve as crutches in moments of discomfort, so too can spending. That phrase—"retail therapy"—isn't always said with a wink. Sometimes it's closer to a confession. The high of a purchase, particularly in environments engineered to trigger dopamine surges, offers a fleeting sense of empowerment. Of course, the come-down often arrives just as quickly, laced with regret or unease.

Here, the language of trauma offers a revealing lens. Many of us are, quite literally, caught in financial trauma responses. Much like the body responds to threat with fight, flight, freeze, or fawn, it can react to money stress in eerily similar ways. A surprise bill might send someone into panic or shutdown. A conversation about debt could spark shame or avoidance. A promising investment might be declined, not because it lacks potential, but because it echoes some deep-rooted narrative of danger or inadequacy. These responses aren't signs of weakness or incompetence. They're adaptations—self-protective responses shaped by past instability, scarcity, or shame, often stretching back decades.

Take Julian, for instance. A gifted graphic designer in his thirties, Julian earns a respectable income and keeps a modest cushion in savings. Yet each time he checks his account balance, his stomach knots. His chest tightens. He avoids opening his banking app for weeks at a time. It's not about numbers—it's about his nervous system. Raised in a home where eviction was a real and recurring threat, his body has learned to associate finances with peril. Even now, with no immediate threat in sight, his physiology hasn't caught up. Budgeting apps can't touch this kind of fear. Because the dissonance isn't in the maths—it's in the memory.

On the opposite end of the spectrum lies something equally paralysing: guilt saving. This pattern often emerges in individuals who've risen from environments of hardship, poverty, or systemic limitation. Even when they've "made it," emotionally speaking, they remain tethered to old scripts. Spending—even modestly, even joyfully—feels indulgent, or worse, morally dubious. The inner dialogue is subtle but punishing: "Do I really need this?" "What if everything disappears tomorrow?" "Shouldn't I be saving instead?" What masquerades as discipline may in fact be a form of self-denial, rooted not in wisdom, but in internalised scarcity.

Aisha's story illustrates this poignantly. A high-achieving medical professional, Aisha grew up wearing hand-me-downs and navigating grocery queues lined with benefit vouchers. Now financially secure, she still struggles to buy anything that doesn't fall into the category of strict utility. When she finally booked a long-overdue holiday abroad, she spent most of the trip wrestling with anxiety and a gnawing sense of guilt. Not because she overspent. But because, at a core level, she believed comfort was something one must perpetually earn—never simply enjoy. The crime, as her nervous system saw it, was not extravagance. It was ease.

So how do we shift these entrenched emotional patterns? Not through austerity. Not by doubling down on budgets or berating ourselves into better habits. The transformation must begin, and be sustained, through emotional intelligence. Willpower alone cannot override the nervous system. Emotional literacy—the ability to recognise, regulate, and respond to inner states—is essential. This includes learning to pause before reacting, to check in with one's body, to discern between a true need and a triggered impulse. And, perhaps most challengingly, to offer compassion to the parts of ourselves that are still responding to threats that no longer exist.

One deceptively simple, yet deeply effective, practice is the somatic check-in. Before making a financial decision—particularly one that feels charged—ask yourself: What's happening in my body right now? Is there tension? Numbness? Excitement? Is the urge to buy coming from desire or distress? This practice isn't about judging the answer. It's about creating a space for awareness. And over time, these moments of awareness become micro-interruptions in the cycle of reactive spending—gradually reprogramming the brain-body association between money and emotional regulation.

Journaling can also serve as a subtle, yet powerful mirror. Not just logging transactions, but mapping the emotional terrain that preceded them. What were you feeling before you bought that gadget? Who were you trying to be when you upgraded your wardrobe? Were you trying to soothe loneliness, assert identity, escape boredom? With enough curiosity—and without self-judgement—patterns begin to emerge. From there, alternative responses can be developed. Perhaps what you needed wasn't a new pair of shoes, but a conversation, a walk, a moment of rest.

Another cornerstone of emotional-financial integration is the shift from reaction to regulation. True financial resilience isn't about banishing fear or impulse; it's about remaining grounded and deliberate even when those feelings arise. One practical method is the pause-and-plan technique. When faced with a decision that evokes stress or urgency, pause. Breathe. Step back. Give yourself a specific, contained plan—be it waiting 24 hours before purchasing, revisiting your goals, or seeking perspective from someone you trust. This brief interruption gives your prefrontal cortex—the brain's reasoning centre—a chance to re-engage, displacing the grip of the stress response.

Miguel, a small business owner, found this particularly transformative. Having grown up with unpredictable finances, he had a habit of splurging during boom months—new gadgets, office upgrades—only to spiral into panic when revenue dipped. By imposing a 48-hour rule on all non-essential spending, Miguel inserted a circuit-breaker into his behaviour. He coupled this with a monthly ritual of reviewing not just his accounts, but his emotional state. Over time, his relationship with money evolved. His choices became more deliberate, his stress less volatile. Not because his income stabilised—but because he did.

The larger truth here is one we don't hear often enough: financial health is deeply entangled with nervous system health. Until we learn to calm the body, understand our emotional responses, and unpick inherited scripts, no amount of income or financial literacy will bring peace. Emotional spending, guilt saving, chronic avoidance—these aren't character defects. They are the body's best attempts to cope. But with attention, compassion, and consistency, they can be reshaped. They can become something softer, wiser—something that supports rather than sabotages.

That is the invitation of this chapter. Not to moralise or pathologise, but to invite you into a new kind of financial awareness—one that honours both the numbers and the nervous system. Emotional intelligence and financial literacy are not opposing skills; they are partners. Together, they create not just control over money, but a deep, grounded freedom in how we experience it.

Because, in the end, money is never only about what we have. It reflects how we feel about what we have. It mirrors back our beliefs, our wounds, our hopes. And when we learn to read that reflection with discernment—and respond with intention—we unlock a wealth that extends far beyond the balance sheet.

Money as a Coping Mechanism

Beneath the surface of what appear to be ordinary purchases lies a world of psychological nuance. A new pair of shoes, a late-night takeaway, or even a sudden weekend getaway may, at first glance, look like lifestyle choices. But frequently, these transactions serve a secondary, and often more significant, purpose: emotional regulation. In these moments, money becomes more than a medium of exchange—it becomes a coping mechanism. It is the tool we reach for not only to acquire goods or experiences, but to soothe distress, assert identity, stave off loneliness, or buffer shame.

Emotional spending is commonly mischaracterised as frivolous or irrational. Yet this interpretation fails to appreciate the underlying intelligence of the behaviour. In psychological terms, coping mechanisms are strategies—conscious or unconscious—that individuals use to manage stress, discomfort, or perceived threat. They are not inherently good or bad; their value depends on context and consequence. When money is used to regulate mood or reassert control in a world that often feels uncertain, it serves an immediate emotional function. The trouble arises when this function becomes habitual, unexamined, and ultimately misaligned with long-term well-being.

To understand emotional spending as a form of self-soothing, we must first acknowledge the emotional landscapes it seeks to navigate. For many, spending becomes a way to disrupt negative affect—stress, anxiety, sadness, boredom, or even existential unease. The act of buying, particularly in digital environments where algorithms anticipate desire, delivers a burst of dopamine—a neurochemical associated with reward and pleasure. This neurobiological reinforcement creates a link between the act of spending and emotional relief, encouraging repetition. Over time, this creates a behavioural pattern in which purchases are not prompted by need, but by emotional discomfort.

Consider the example of Leila, a corporate professional who frequently found herself browsing online retailers after work. On days of high stress or conflict with colleagues, her cart would grow heavier. The packages would arrive in neat cardboard boxes, offering momentary excitement and the illusion of agency. Yet within hours—sometimes minutes—the buzz would fade, replaced by guilt and confusion. Rationally, Leila knew she did not need the items. But emotionally, she was responding to a deeply conditioned association between consumption and comfort. Her financial decisions were not reflective of poor discipline—they were responses to unprocessed tension.

Another layer of emotional spending is validation-seeking. This is particularly evident in social media-driven cultures, where identity is increasingly tied to aesthetics, experiences, and material signals. Spending becomes a way to project success, belonging, or desirability—externally visible markers that compensate for internal uncertainty. When someone books an expensive meal, not for pleasure but for the photograph, or purchases clothing that reflects aspirational rather than authentic style, what they are often seeking is approval. Money, in this context, becomes a form of language: a way of saying *I matter* or *I'm enough*.

This dynamic is not limited to the young or image-conscious. Javier, a middle-aged entrepreneur, admitted that he often leased luxury cars despite inconsistent income. For him, driving a high-status vehicle was a way to protect his image—both to others and to himself—after a string of professional setbacks. It was not about the car, but about reassurance. His spending was a psychological scaffold, holding up a sense of self that felt increasingly fragile.

Avoidance is another powerful driver of emotionally motivated financial behaviour. For many, engaging with money—through budgeting, debt management, or investment planning—triggers intense discomfort. This may be due to early experiences of financial instability, shame, or a lack of financial education. To avoid these feelings, individuals often engage in patterns that create the illusion of engagement without the discomfort of accountability. These might include spontaneous giving, undirected saving, or compulsive paying down of small debts while ignoring larger obligations. In each case, the behaviour allows the person to feel active without confronting the source of their anxiety.

Take Ananya, a freelance writer who compulsively paid off her credit card in full every few days, even when the balance was negligible. While this may appear responsible on the surface, her motivation was not financial hygiene but emotional control. Ananya had grown up watching her parents drown in debt, and any outstanding balance—even a few pounds—activated feelings of panic. Her behaviour was a way to suppress those emotions, not to optimise her cash flow. In avoiding one set of feelings, she inadvertently created another: chronic financial vigilance, which led to burnout and decision fatigue.

Understanding money as a coping mechanism does not require us to vilify spending or pathologise emotion. Rather, it invites us to examine intention. When we spend to soothe, validate, or avoid, we must ask—*what am I really trying to feel?* and *is there a more aligned way to meet that need?* This is not about austerity. It is about awareness.

One practical approach to increasing this awareness is what financial psychologists call "emotional tagging." Before making a discretionary purchase, pause to name the emotion you're currently feeling. Is it loneliness, boredom, shame, elation, or fear? Then ask yourself whether the purchase is likely to resolve that feeling in a sustainable way. Often, the pause itself is enough to bring clarity. If the desire persists, the purchase may be grounded in genuine value. If it dissipates, it was likely a proxy for something else.

Another effective method is to track spending through an emotional lens rather than a categorical one. Traditional budgeting asks you to assign purchases to fixed categories—groceries, travel, entertainment. Emotional budgeting asks: *what state was I in when I spent this money?* Over time, patterns emerge. You may discover that late-night spending is driven by anxiety, or that purchases after social events are linked to feelings of exclusion. These patterns are rich with insight. They reveal not just how you spend, but *why* you spend.

Crucially, this work must be done without shame. Emotional spending, like emotional eating or emotional silence, is a form of adaptation. It deserves compassion, not condemnation. But it also demands evolution. If money has become a default tool for emotional regulation, then part of financial maturity involves expanding your toolkit—developing alternative strategies for comfort, control, and connection.

This might mean cultivating rituals of emotional regulation that do not involve spending: journaling after stressful meetings, taking a walk before checking out an online cart, or reaching out to a friend before making a high-cost decision. It might also mean redefining what self-care and reward look like. A massage or a gourmet meal can be entirely appropriate forms of celebration. But when they are substitutes for emotional presence, they become expensive detours rather than affirming destinations.

At its best, money can enhance well-being. But when used habitually as a coping mechanism, it can erode both financial and emotional health. The work, then, is not to eliminate emotionality from money, but to integrate it wisely. This requires curiosity, consistency, and courage. It means being willing to sit with discomfort long enough to understand it, rather than rushing to silence it with a transaction.

Ultimately, the invitation is not to stop spending, but to spend from a place of clarity rather than compulsion, alignment rather than avoidance. When you understand the emotional architecture behind your financial habits, you begin to reclaim your agency. You stop outsourcing your emotional needs to your bank account. And in that space—between stimulus and response—you begin to craft a new relationship with money: one that honours your feelings, supports your goals, and reflects not your fears, but your values.

The Physiology of Financial Stress

Financial stress is not a metaphorical condition—it is a physiological state. While discussions around money often focus on external metrics—income, debt, expenses—what remains less visible, but equally influential, is how our bodies respond to financial stimuli. The elevated heart rate at the sight of an overdue bill. The pit in the stomach after checking a depleted account. The paralysis when asked to speak to a financial advisor. These are not imagined responses; they are embodied experiences. At the intersection of psychology, neuroscience, and trauma research lies a compelling insight: our nervous system reacts to financial threat in much the same way it reacts to physical danger.

This chapter introduces the concept of the *money trauma response*—a physiological reaction to perceived financial threat that engages the body's ancient survival mechanisms: fight, flight, freeze, or fawn. These responses, originally evolved to protect us from predators and mortal harm, are now triggered by modern stressors such as mounting debt, insecure income, or the social consequences of perceived financial failure. Understanding this biological backdrop is essential not only for navigating personal finance with greater awareness, but for dismantling the shame so often entangled with financial dysfunction.

The human nervous system, when faced with threat, defaults to the autonomic response: a cascade of neurochemical changes that prepare the body to either confront the threat or escape it. When this response is activated by money-related stimuli, the body does not distinguish between a missed mortgage payment and a physical attack. It floods the system with adrenaline and cortisol, tightens muscles, increases vigilance, and impairs executive function. In other words, it becomes harder to think clearly, make reasoned decisions, or engage in long-term planning—just when those skills are most needed.

Consider the case of Priya, a freelance illustrator who was raised in a household where financial unpredictability was the norm. Although she now earns a respectable income, any deviation in cash flow—such as a delayed payment—triggers panic. She finds herself catastrophising: *"What if I can't pay rent? What if I lose all my clients? What if I end up back where I started?"* In these moments, she cannot focus on client work, avoids emails, and loses sleep. Her body enters a sustained stress response that far exceeds the practical reality of the situation. The trigger is financial, but the response is biological.

The fight response in financial terms can manifest as confrontational or impulsive behaviours: overcorrecting by slashing expenses dramatically, angrily disputing charges, or making aggressive decisions such as pulling investments prematurely or quitting a job out of frustration. The body is flooded with cortisol, the stress hormone that sharpens focus temporarily but impairs long-term reasoning. These actions are rarely strategic—they are reactive, driven by a nervous system trying to restore a sense of control.

Flight, on the other hand, often presents as avoidance. This can look like delaying tax returns, ignoring bank statements, or putting off necessary conversations about money. People in a flight state may obsessively move from one financial tool or strategy to another without commitment, constantly searching for a way to feel safe. Behind the procrastination is not laziness, but physiological overwhelm. The brain's prefrontal cortex, responsible for planning and logic, is effectively hijacked by the limbic system, which prioritises survival over strategy.

Freeze responses are characterised by shutdown and paralysis. This is the person who opens a letter from their bank and immediately feels numb. Who stops answering phone calls from creditors. Who avoids thinking about money altogether because doing so triggers a flood of helplessness. Freeze is not apathy—it is a nervous system response to perceived inescapability. In this state, even the smallest financial task can feel insurmountable, further entrenching patterns of dysfunction.

Fawn, a less widely discussed but equally significant response, involves appeasing others to avoid conflict or rejection. In financial contexts, this may look like consistently undercharging for services, agreeing to expenses out of social pressure, or financially overextending oneself to maintain approval. The individual may appear generous or compliant, but the underlying motive is often fear of abandonment or conflict. This response is common among individuals with a history of trauma or high relational sensitivity, where financial boundaries are sacrificed in the service of perceived safety.

These patterns are not merely behavioural—they are somatic. They live in the body, often reinforced over years or even decades. People who grew up in environments of chronic scarcity, instability, or financial shame may find that their nervous systems have been primed for hyperarousal in money-related situations. The body remembers what the mind tries to forget. Even when financial conditions improve, the physiological response remains unless it is consciously addressed.

Understanding the physiology of financial stress allows us to shift from moralising to empathising. A person who cannot face their bank account is not weak; they are dysregulated. A person who spends impulsively after a period of deprivation is not irresponsible; they are attempting to restore nervous system equilibrium. When we recognise these responses for what they are—automatic, adaptive mechanisms—we can begin to meet them not with judgment, but with regulation.

Practical applications of this insight begin with self-awareness. Noticing how your body responds to financial cues is the first step. Do you feel tightness in your chest when thinking about debt? Does your heart rate increase when discussing salary? Do you experience mental fog when trying to budget? These are signals from your nervous system—not signs that you are broken, but that your body is reacting to learned associations.

Interventions should begin not with spreadsheets, but with somatic grounding. Techniques such as slow, diaphragmatic breathing, progressive muscle relaxation, or even brief walks can help bring the nervous system out of threat mode and into a state of relative safety. Only from this place can higher-order thinking resume. It is in this state that budgeting becomes tolerable, planning becomes possible, and dialogue becomes constructive.

Working with a trauma-informed financial coach or therapist can further support this process. These professionals understand that money is not just math—it is memory, emotion, and identity. They can help clients trace the roots of their responses, reframe disempowering narratives, and build strategies that honour both the emotional and practical dimensions of financial life.

This does not mean abandoning financial literacy. On the contrary, combining it with nervous system literacy is what enables sustainable transformation. It's the difference between knowing you *should* invest and feeling safe enough to do so. Between understanding that debt reduction matters and having the regulation to face the plan without overwhelm. Between recognising that boundaries are important and being able to hold them when challenged.

Financial resilience, therefore, is not simply a matter of knowledge—it is a matter of regulation. It is the capacity to remain grounded in the face of financial stress, to respond rather than react, and to hold financial discomfort without collapsing into fear-based behaviours. This kind of resilience is not taught in schools, yet it underpins every financial decision we make.

We live in a culture that often celebrates financial competence while ignoring the emotional and physiological realities that make it possible. By integrating the language of trauma and nervous system response into our financial conversations, we create space for a more humane, inclusive, and effective approach to money. One that honours not only our cognitive strategies, but our lived experiences. One that sees the whole person—not just the bottom line.

Ultimately, the goal is not to eliminate financial stress entirely—that would be unrealistic and, perhaps, undesirable. A degree of stress can be motivating and clarifying. But when stress becomes chronic and dysregulating, it undermines the very progress we seek. By learning to understand and regulate our physiological responses, we reclaim agency. We begin to move through financial life not as a battleground of fear, but as a field of conscious, embodied choice. And in doing so, we lay the foundation for a new kind of wealth—one rooted not only in assets and income, but in calm, clarity, and inner safety.

Healing the Guilt of Spending

For many who have risen from a background of financial scarcity, the act of spending—even modestly, even wisely—does not feel like liberation. It feels like betrayal. The moment that should bring pleasure or affirmation instead brings unease, hesitation, or outright guilt. A well-earned holiday triggers second-guessing. A quality pair of shoes, chosen with care, induces discomfort. A celebratory meal after a promotion ends not with satisfaction, but with an internalised reprimand: *Do I really deserve this?* This guilt is rarely about the money itself. Rather, it is about the unconscious inheritance of beliefs shaped by early exposure to lack.

Spending guilt is a deeply layered emotional phenomenon. It often afflicts those who have worked hard to build financial stability, yet find themselves emotionally unprepared to enjoy the fruits of their labour. At its root is a form of psychological dissonance—the internal narrative formed in an environment of scarcity colliding with the external reality of sufficiency. The mind has moved forward; the nervous system has not. And until both align, even the most rational, deserved, and strategic purchases can provoke discomfort.

To understand this tension, we must begin by looking at the formative role that early financial environments play in shaping our emotional relationship with money. Childhoods marked by frugality, unpredictability, or outright deprivation condition individuals to associate spending with danger. In such households, every discretionary purchase might have been met with anxiety or judgement. Parents may have argued over costs, sacrificed their own needs, or shamed children for "wanting too much." These messages, whether explicit or implicit, become internalised as enduring truths: *Money must be stretched. Luxuries are wasteful. Enjoyment is indulgence. Safety lies in sacrifice.*

These beliefs persist even after financial circumstances improve. Take the example of Dev, a first-generation university graduate who now earns a six-figure salary in the tech sector. Despite his success, Dev struggles to make non-essential purchases. When he finally allowed himself to buy a new laptop—after years of overextending an ageing device—he returned it days later, convinced it was too extravagant. The decision wasn't financial; he had budgeted for the expense. The discomfort came from violating a script embedded in childhood: *Spend only on what is strictly necessary, and nothing more.* For Dev, sufficiency felt unsafe because his emotional conditioning had equated spending with loss.

This internal conflict is further intensified by survivor's guilt—a common experience among those who have surpassed the economic standing of their families or communities. Spending, in this context, becomes not just a financial act but a symbolic distancing. Buying the more expensive brand, booking the holiday abroad, or eating at a high-end restaurant can trigger a sense of disloyalty, as though one is leaving behind those who still live with constraint. The emotional logic whispers: *If they're struggling, how can I allow myself comfort?* What masquerades as virtue is often a misplaced form of allegiance.

Women, in particular, often face intensified layers of this guilt. Conditioned to prioritise others, to minimise their own needs, and to justify every expense in terms of utility or sacrifice, many find it difficult to spend on themselves without emotional friction. A mother might hesitate to buy a new coat because the children need school supplies. A professional woman might downplay her desire for a tailored suit, convincing herself she can "make do" with what she has. In both cases, the guilt is not about money. It's about socialised beliefs around worthiness and care.

Healing this form of guilt begins with recognising that it is not irrational—it is relational. The guilt does not emerge from an inability to calculate affordability. It emerges from the dissonance between past identity and present reality. The nervous system, habituated to scarcity, flags abundance as unsafe. But with attention and practice, it is possible to retrain these patterns and cultivate an internal sense of safety around spending.

The first step is conscious reframing. When guilt arises, it can be helpful to ask: *Whose voice is this? Whose values am I embodying right now? Is this belief still relevant to the life I lead today?* Often, the guilt is an echo from the past—parents, teachers, or cultural norms—rather than a reflection of present needs or values. Bringing awareness to the source of the guilt allows one to hold it with compassion rather than confusion.

One powerful tool for this work is financial affirmation grounded in personal values. Rather than countering guilt with hollow positivity, individuals can construct affirmations that integrate past experience with present empowerment. For instance, someone might affirm: *I honour the sacrifices of my past by spending wisely and joyfully in the present.* Or: *I deserve to enjoy what I have built with integrity and care.* These statements do not deny history; they contextualise it within a broader narrative of growth.

Embodying these new narratives often requires action. Gradual, intentional spending on meaningful items or experiences can help recalibrate the nervous system. This might involve setting a "joy fund"—a dedicated account or category for spending that reflects self-care, creativity, or celebration. The act of allocating money to joy, and then spending it without guilt, becomes a behavioural signal to the brain: *It is safe to have. It is safe to enjoy. It is safe to be well.* With repetition, these actions begin to overwrite old associations.

Therapeutic support can also be immensely helpful, particularly for those whose spending guilt is rooted in trauma or family systems marked by enmeshment or emotional manipulation. Family-of-origin dynamics often assign roles such as "the provider," "the selfless one," or "the caretaker," all of which can conflict with personal financial freedom. A therapist trained in financial psychology or trauma-informed approaches can help unpack these roles and facilitate healthier boundaries.

Beyond the individual level, this work also requires a cultural reckoning. Societies that moralise frugality and romanticise self-denial often pathologise financial pleasure. The script that equates worth with struggle, or virtue with deprivation, is not only outdated—it is harmful. A healthy economy, like a healthy psyche, must allow space for both restraint and enjoyment. To spend with joy is not to betray one's values; it is to express them. To feel safe in sufficiency is not to forget hardship; it is to honour it by breaking cycles of deprivation.

This is especially important in intergenerational contexts. Children of those who lived through war, colonisation, or systemic poverty often carry inherited narratives of fear. When they begin to live differently, their behaviour challenges the emotional logic of the previous generation. This can create tension—but also opportunity. By healing their own guilt, they model for others what it means to thrive without shame, to enjoy without apology, and to lead with both gratitude and grace.

Ultimately, healing the guilt of spending is about learning to trust oneself again. Trust that you are capable of discernment. Trust that your values, not your fears, can guide your financial choices. Trust that enjoying what you have does not diminish your empathy for others, but deepens it. When guilt is replaced with grounded permission, a different kind of wealth emerges—not merely financial, but emotional. The wealth of ease, of self-trust, of being at home in your own life.

This is not about abandoning the lessons of scarcity, but about evolving them. It is about shifting from hypervigilance to discernment, from guilt to gratitude, and from internalised struggle to embodied sufficiency. And when that shift occurs—quietly, consistently, and courageously—spending becomes not a source of shame, but a celebration of healing, growth, and the rightful enjoyment of a life well-earned.

Emotional Intelligence for Everyday Money Moves

In the world of personal finance, intelligence is often measured in numbers—credit scores, income brackets, asset portfolios. Yet what truly determines our financial well-being, especially in daily decision-making, is not how much we know but how well we manage our emotions in relation to money. This is the domain of financial emotional intelligence, or financial EQ: the capacity to perceive, understand, and regulate one's emotional responses to financial situations. And it is arguably more important than any budgeting app or investment strategy.

Financial EQ is not a soft skill—it is a foundational one. It enables us to pause before making an impulse purchase, to negotiate without self-sabotage, to sit with discomfort without reaching for a quick-fix expense. Without it, even the most informed individuals can find themselves derailed by emotional triggers, relational dynamics, or unconscious scripts. With it, clarity, confidence, and resilience become possible—not just theoretically, but in the very moment that counts: when decisions are made, money is spent, and habits are reinforced.

At its core, emotional intelligence consists of five components: self-awareness, self-regulation, motivation, empathy, and social skills. When applied to finance, these components allow us to do more than balance budgets—they help us align our money behaviours with our values, navigate difficult conversations, and respond rather than react to stress. Building this capacity is not about suppressing emotion. It is about learning to integrate emotional information into rational decision-making.

One of the most practical ways to begin developing financial EQ is by learning the art of the pause. In a culture that privileges immediacy—one-click orders, rapid digital payments, real-time offers—pausing is a radical act. Yet a brief moment of interruption between impulse and action can significantly alter the trajectory of a financial choice. Pausing before making a purchase, particularly one driven by emotion, allows the nervous system to settle and the rational brain to re-engage. This small delay enables a key question to arise: *What am I feeling, and what do I actually need?*

Take the example of Darren, a marketing executive who found himself repeatedly shopping online after stressful workdays. While he initially believed these purchases were harmless rewards, a pattern of clutter and credit card debt told a different story. By introducing a self-imposed "one-hour pause" rule for any non-essential purchases, Darren created space to interrogate his feelings—frustration, inadequacy, fatigue—and to find other ways to meet those needs, such as calling a friend or going for a walk. Over time, his spending became more intentional, not because he developed greater willpower, but because he built the habit of emotional inquiry.

Journaling is another powerful technique for enhancing financial self-awareness. It transforms money management from a purely cognitive task into a reflective practice. When used consistently, journaling can uncover patterns, reveal triggers, and offer a safe space to examine the emotional undercurrents of financial decisions. Prompts such as *"What does this purchase represent to me?"*, *"What money stories am I acting out today?"*, or *"What feelings am I trying to avoid through spending or withholding?"* can yield insights far deeper than any spreadsheet.

Journaling is particularly effective when paired with regular check-ins. These check-ins need not be lengthy. Even five minutes at the end of the day, reviewing your financial actions alongside your emotional state, can help reinforce awareness and self-trust. For example, acknowledging a moment of restraint—choosing not to buy something impulsively—and reflecting on how it felt emotionally reinforces positive behaviour at both a cognitive and somatic level.

Speaking of the body, it is impossible to develop financial EQ without attending to the nervous system. Somatic check-ins—the practice of noticing physical sensations and interpreting them as emotional cues—offer an often-overlooked layer of intelligence. The body frequently registers stress before the mind does. Tightness in the chest when opening a bank statement, shallow breathing during a salary negotiation, or a fluttering stomach when deciding whether to invest—these are all signals. The question is whether we heed them.

Somatic literacy helps individuals distinguish between real financial constraints and perceived threats rooted in past experience. Someone raised in a household where money was always scarce might feel anxiety at any form of spending, even when it is well within budget. Without somatic awareness, that anxiety can be mistaken for a warning, leading to unnecessary restriction or guilt. With awareness, the individual can acknowledge the sensation, trace it to its origin, and decide whether it reflects the present moment. Over time, this practice fosters emotional neutrality around money—replacing panic with perspective.

Building financial EQ also enhances relational money dynamics. Empathy, one of emotional intelligence's core pillars, becomes critical in navigating shared finances, family expectations, or cultural pressures. Being able to recognise not only your own emotional patterns but those of a partner, parent, or colleague allows for more constructive dialogue and less reactive conflict. Rather than escalating a disagreement about spending, an empathetic approach might sound like: *"I hear that you're feeling uncertain about this expense. Can we talk about what security looks like for both of us?"* Such language shifts the conversation from binary judgments to collaborative problem-solving.

Financial EQ also supports long-term motivation, especially in the face of delayed gratification. Saving for retirement, reducing debt, or building an emergency fund requires the ability to connect present behaviour with future benefit. This connection is not purely logical—it is emotional. Emotionally intelligent individuals are able to visualise and emotionally invest in future outcomes, making it easier to resist short-term temptations. They cultivate what psychologists call "future self-continuity"—the sense that their future self is not a stranger, but someone worth caring for.

Sophia, a schoolteacher working towards financial independence, exemplified this principle. Initially, she struggled to stick to her savings goals, often dipping into her emergency fund for discretionary purchases. After working with a coach to develop visual representations of her future goals—images of the home she wanted to buy, letters to her future self, and even voice notes—she found herself more emotionally invested in long-term outcomes. Her savings rate increased, not because she became more frugal, but because she had strengthened her emotional bond with her future self.

This capacity to hold dual emotional truths—to appreciate present desires while honouring future intentions—is a hallmark of financial maturity. It allows individuals to make money decisions that are not reactive, but responsive. Not binary, but balanced. Not emotionally detached, but emotionally integrated.

To cultivate such maturity is not a one-time effort. It is a practice, a series of small, consistent choices that build emotional capacity and financial competence simultaneously. It is pausing when tempted. Reflecting when triggered. Listening to the body. Naming the feeling. Choosing the aligned action. And doing it again, not perfectly, but deliberately.

Financial education must evolve to reflect this complexity. It is no longer enough to teach compound interest or tax deductions without also addressing fear, shame, identity, and trauma. Financial literacy and emotional intelligence are not separate domains—they are two sides of the same ledger. When taught together, they unlock not just fiscal responsibility, but personal sovereignty.

Ultimately, financial EQ invites us into a more conscious relationship with money—one where emotions are not liabilities to be avoided, but signals to be understood. Where spending, saving, giving, and earning are not just acts of accounting, but expressions of values, boundaries, and self-worth. And where each everyday decision becomes an opportunity to practice presence, build trust, and shape a financial life that is not only sustainable, but deeply satisfying.

From Reaction to Regulation: Building Resilience in Financial Decision-Making

At the centre of every financial choice is a nervous system responding to perceived risk, value, and consequence. Whether we are negotiating a raise, contemplating a large purchase, or facing unexpected bills, the body is not passive in these moments. It reacts—often swiftly and silently—before the mind has had time to fully process the decision at hand. In these high-stakes instances, the difference between a financially wise decision and a reactive one often lies in a person's ability to regulate their nervous system. Building that capacity for regulation is not a luxury of the emotionally enlightened—it is a practical necessity for anyone who seeks to make sustainable, values-aligned financial choices.

The human nervous system evolved to prioritise survival. When it detects threat, real or perceived, it initiates a cascade of physiological responses—heart rate accelerates, digestion slows, blood flow is redirected, and the brain's higher-order reasoning functions are deprioritised in favour of fast, protective action. This system served our ancestors well in life-or-death situations. But in modern financial contexts, where perceived danger often relates to social standing, emotional safety, or long-term security rather than physical harm, this same physiological alarm system can misfire. It can drive us to overspend, under-earn, avoid budgeting, or panic-sell investments—not because the numbers demand it, but because our bodies do.

Understanding this biological architecture is the first step toward transformation. The fight, flight, freeze, and fawn responses—so central to trauma theory—are frequently activated in financial situations. Someone receiving a debt collection letter might go into fight mode, engaging aggressively with a customer service agent, or flight mode, ignoring the issue entirely. Freeze may manifest as paralysis around money decisions, where even opening a banking app feels overwhelming. Fawn might appear in someone who overcommits financially to please others, sacrificing their own needs in the process. In each case, the person is not making an informed choice—they are reacting from a dysregulated state.

Take the example of Sarah, a non-profit executive with a long-standing pattern of financial avoidance. Although competent and respected in her professional life, she found it difficult to face her personal finances. Each month, she delayed opening bills, avoided checking her accounts, and postponed tax preparation. When she finally did engage with her finances, it was in a flurry of anxiety and dread. Through coaching and nervous system education, Sarah came to recognise her pattern as a freeze response—rooted not in incompetence, but in a childhood shaped by financial volatility and fear. With this insight, she began practising regulation techniques before engaging with money tasks. Over time, what once felt like an existential threat became a manageable routine.

This movement—from reaction to regulation—is the crux of financial resilience. It does not eliminate emotional responses to money, nor should it. Emotions contain valuable information about our values, boundaries, and needs. But unregulated emotions distort perception, collapse perspective, and limit access to the prefrontal cortex—the part of the brain responsible for logical reasoning, impulse control, and future planning. In moments of financial decision-making, it is essential that we learn to recognise when our nervous system has been hijacked, and to bring ourselves back into a state of calm before acting.

There are several practical tools that support this shift, each grounded in research from neuroscience, somatic psychology, and behavioural economics. One of the most accessible is intentional breathing. Slow, diaphragmatic breathing has been shown to activate the parasympathetic nervous system—the body's rest-and-digest mode—which counteracts the stress response. A person facing a high-stakes financial conversation might pause for two minutes of slow breathing, consciously exhaling longer than they inhale. This signals safety to the body and brings executive function back online.

Another tool is orienting. This somatic technique involves physically looking around the environment, naming objects or colours, and bringing attention to the body's contact with the ground or chair. It may seem unrelated to money at first glance, but it re-establishes a sense of present-moment safety. Many people report that even a few moments of orienting before checking their bank account dramatically reduces anticipatory anxiety and the urge to dissociate or react impulsively.

Body-based practices are not replacements for financial strategy; they are enablers of it. They allow us to access the cognitive clarity required to implement budgeting systems, investment plans, or debt repayment schedules. Without nervous system regulation, even the most well-crafted financial plan remains aspirational. With regulation, those same tools become actionable.

For Aaron, a start-up founder navigating volatile income and high personal risk, regulation became a strategic asset. In the early stages of his business, Aaron found himself making decisions from a place of emotional reactivity—hiring out of panic, underpricing his services, or overcompensating during downturns. By learning to track his physiological signals—tightness in the chest, shallow breath, clenched jaw—he began to notice when he was entering a dysregulated state. Instead of pushing through, he would step away, practise a regulation technique, and return when calm. His decisions improved. So did his results.

The shift from reaction to regulation also enhances interpersonal financial dynamics. Couples, business partners, or family members frequently bring different nervous system responses to money. One may react with urgency, another with avoidance. Without mutual understanding of these patterns, conflict escalates. But when both parties learn to name their physiological states and take a moment to regulate before responding, conversations become more constructive. What was once a trigger becomes an invitation for co-regulation—a shared process of grounding and listening.

Regulation also helps to interrupt shame cycles. Many individuals carry financial shame—guilt over debt, embarrassment about spending habits, or regret over past mistakes. These emotions often lead to self-recrimination and further avoidance, perpetuating the cycle. Regulation techniques offer a compassionate interruption. They remind us that shame is not a call to punishment, but a signal for care. A regulated body can sit with shame without collapsing into it, allowing for repair, reflection, and recommitment.

Building financial resilience through regulation does not require perfection. There will still be moments of emotional reaction—sudden expenses, unexpected downturns, tense discussions. But the goal is not to eliminate reactivity; it is to reduce its duration and intensity. The faster we can recognise a dysregulated state, the faster we can return to clarity. This capacity builds over time, through practice, reflection, and self-trust.

Incorporating regulation into everyday financial routines creates a foundation of safety. Begin with small rituals: a grounding breath before opening emails, a five-minute walk before reviewing a budget, a body scan before initiating a difficult financial conversation. These moments build internal muscle memory. The body learns, over time, that financial engagement is not a threat. It becomes familiar. It becomes safe.

This work is especially powerful for those with a history of financial trauma—individuals who grew up in poverty, experienced economic instability, or inherited disempowering beliefs about money. For them, regulation is not a nicety; it is a necessity. It creates the psychological space to reauthor their financial story—not as one of perpetual survival, but of sovereign choice.

Ultimately, the path from reaction to regulation is about reclaiming agency. It is about choosing how to engage with money, rather than being controlled by unconscious patterns. It is about building a relationship with your nervous system that supports your financial goals, rather than undermines them. And it is about recognising that true financial well-being is not just a matter of numbers—it is a matter of presence.

When the body is calm, the mind is clear. And when the mind is clear, money becomes not a battlefield, but a tool—one you can use with discernment, direction, and integrity. In this regulated state, financial resilience is not merely possible; it becomes inevitable.

Chapter 5
The Language of Money and Mental Wealth

Money isn't just counted—it's conjured. Not in the mystical sense, but in the way language weaves itself around value, subtly shaping how we experience and express wealth. The words we use when speaking about money, whether muttered under our breath or shared aloud, carry weight far beyond their syllables. They form a kind of operating system for our beliefs and behaviours, scripting the roles we play and the ceilings we don't realise we're reinforcing. In this light, language is no idle accessory—it's a creative force, a kind of currency itself.

Much of what we call a scarcity mindset is, at its roots, a linguistic habit. It's astonishing how frequently a phrase like "I'm broke" or "I'll never be good with money" slips from our mouths without a second thought. But these aren't harmless throwaways—they're incantations of lack. Every repetition etches the belief a little deeper into our nervous systems. Over time, such phrases harden into psychological walls, not just describing a financial reality but fortifying it. It's the grammar of limitation, masquerading as realism.

There's ample psychological footing for this notion. Cognitive behavioural therapy, for instance, hinges on the understanding that our thoughts shape our emotions, and our emotions, in turn, guide our actions. Language is how thought becomes tangible. When we continually label ourselves as "hopeless with money," we begin to act accordingly—avoiding opportunities, shying away from growth, tuning out information that contradicts our narrative. It becomes a feedback loop: identity fuels language, language shapes perception, perception governs behaviour.

But there's another layer, one less quantifiable but no less potent. Words have energy. This might sound airy, but consider how differently your body reacts to "I'm working toward financial abundance" versus "I'm always scraping by." One opens the chest. The other tightens it. Expansive language has the curious effect of inviting action—it coaxes us to take risks, make plans, move. Restrictive language does the opposite. It huddles us into caution. It's not about sugar-coating reality, but about choosing a tone that permits possibility.

Take Nadia. She ran a small but capable design business and often referred to herself, affectionately, as a "scrappy underdog." It made her relatable—yes—but also subtly set the tone for how others engaged with her. Prospective clients sensed her modesty and responded in kind: negotiating fees, questioning her positioning. It wasn't until a mentor suggested she describe her business as "boutique consulting" and present herself as a "strategic partner" that things began to shift. The change wasn't just rhetorical. It recalibrated how she saw herself—and how others did too.

Upgrading your financial vocabulary isn't about delusion or puffery. It's about aligning your words with the direction you wish to grow in. That might sound self-evident, yet the resistance is real. There's a comfort in old scripts, even when they constrain us. Replacing "I can't afford this" with "How could I make this work?" isn't denial; it's a redirection. Swapping "I'm bad with money" for "I'm learning to manage my finances more wisely" shifts the focus from failure to process. And "I choose not to spend on that right now" carries agency that "I can't" simply doesn't.

Of course, none of this happens by accident. Rewriting your financial narrative requires attention—and some persistence. One particularly effective approach is money journaling. It's not about documenting transactions; it's about tracking the stories behind them. Questions like "Where did I learn this belief about money?" or "What assumptions do I make when someone talks about wealth?" open up space for excavation. Combine this with a touch of visualisation—imagining what it would feel like to inhabit a more empowered financial identity—and the exercise becomes surprisingly catalytic.

This isn't mere theory. In one financial coaching group, a participant began journaling about her discomfort with accepting payment. Eventually, she uncovered an inherited belief: that to be good was to be self-sacrificing, and money compromised that virtue. She reframed the narrative—something along the lines of, "It is both ethical and wise to receive fair compensation"—and within months, she'd raised her rates and stopped caveating every invoice with an apology. The numbers shifted, yes—but more significantly, so did her sense of self.

It's also worth noting that language doesn't live in a vacuum. What we say to others—partners, clients, peers—either reinforces or disrupts our internal scripts. Speaking your value aloud is one of the simplest yet most confronting acts of self-affirmation. Saying "I want to grow my income this year" to a friend is different from thinking it alone. Declaring "This is my rate" with conviction instead of a rising inflection changes how it's received. Externalising the shift makes it more real.

This becomes especially vital in close relationships. Financial conversations with partners, for example, often derail not because of numbers, but because of unspoken stories. One partner hears "budget" and thinks security; the other hears restriction. When couples catch themselves using phrases like "We always overspend" or "You never care about saving," there's a chance to pause and reframe. A small linguistic shift—from accusation to curiosity—can dissolve tension. Try "What would it look like if we approached this differently?" instead. It's surprising how often tone trumps content.

And in professional life? The way we frame financial matters broadcasts more than we realise. A freelancer who names their rate without flinching often attracts respect. A leader who refers to staff development as an "investment" rather than a "cost" signals vision. These aren't semantic flourishes—they're clues to mindset, and mindset attracts resonance.

Which brings us to the deeper truth at the heart of all this: language is a construction tool. The scaffolding of your financial life is held up not just by spreadsheets or strategies, but by the phrases you habitually reach for. Weak, habitual language builds wobbly foundations. Conscious, empowered language creates sturdier ground—space enough to expand into.

So, the invitation is simple, if not easy: speak differently. Choose words that reflect the person you're becoming, not just the one you've been. Let language be a rehearsal for change, not just a record of past limitations. Each sentence, however small, is a brick. With enough of them, you begin to build.

This chapter, then, isn't just about finding better words. It's about reclaiming authorship. About using language not as camouflage, but as compass. Because in the end, wealth is not only about what we hold—but how we speak of what we hold. And the voice you use to narrate your financial life? That voice is shaping the whole story.

Words Create Wealth (or Wreck It)

The way we speak about money matters more than we often realise. Not simply because language reflects thought, but because language *shapes* it—forming the very architecture of how we perceive, engage with, and ultimately create our financial reality. When a person habitually uses phrases like *"I'm broke," "I'm terrible with money,"* or *"Money just slips through my fingers,"* they are not merely describing a temporary situation—they are reinforcing a belief system that quietly governs their choices. Over time, this language solidifies into a script, and that script becomes a self-fulfilling financial identity.

This phenomenon is what many financial psychologists and behavioural economists refer to as *poverty consciousness*: a persistent mental state marked by feelings of scarcity, fear, limitation, and helplessness, regardless of one's actual income or material conditions. Language is one of the most powerful transmitters of this state. When repeated often enough, even in jest or social mimicry, disempowering financial language does more than signal a lack of confidence—it *cultivates* it. It embeds poverty into the mind before it ever manifests in the bank account.

The relationship between language and identity is well-documented in psychological research. Our self-concept is not a static truth—it is an ongoing narrative we reinforce through the words we use. If that narrative is peppered with phrases like *"I'll never get ahead," "I'm not a money person,"* or *"That's for people like them, not me,"* then the identity that emerges is one of disempowerment. And our behaviour follows suit. We procrastinate on financial planning, underprice our work, avoid investment conversations, or settle for jobs that underpay us—not because we lack ability, but because we've unconsciously taught ourselves not to expect more.

Real-world examples illustrate the potency of these linguistic habits. Consider Maya, a gifted designer who consistently told friends and colleagues, *"I'm just not business-minded."* That one phrase—spoken with a shrug—allowed her to dismiss uncomfortable but necessary tasks like pricing, negotiating, and invoicing. Over time, her income stagnated. It wasn't a matter of talent or demand—both were abundant—but of language. When challenged to reframe her narrative, she began saying, *"I'm learning to run a business in a way that reflects my creativity."* That shift in phrasing allowed her to take a short business course, raise her rates, and engage with money from a place of curiosity rather than avoidance.

The impact of language on behaviour is amplified by the brain's pattern-seeking nature. Through a process known as *cognitive reinforcement*, the brain is constantly scanning for evidence that confirms what we already believe to be true. When we say *"I'm bad with money,"* the brain highlights every financial misstep and downplays every success. It becomes a self-validating loop. Conversely, when we say *"I'm developing new financial habits,"* the brain becomes primed to notice and celebrate progress, no matter how incremental. This is not magical thinking; it is behavioural conditioning informed by decades of psychological research.

There is also a sociocultural layer to this pattern. In many communities, particularly those shaped by systemic inequality, phrases like *"I'm always just getting by"* or *"Money doesn't grow on trees"* serve a dual function: they express lived realities, but they also encode a worldview in which financial struggle is both expected and inevitable. While such expressions may offer temporary solidarity or humour, when internalised without reflection, they risk becoming generational scripts. They teach children not only how to manage money, but how to *think* about money—with limits, with caution, and often with fear.

This is particularly problematic when financial difficulty becomes a source of identity. Identifying as someone who is always *scraping by* may offer a sense of belonging or virtue—*"At least I'm not materialistic"*—but it also reinforces limitation. It creates a ceiling on what one believes is possible or permissible. People may begin to reject financial growth opportunities—not consciously, but because they feel emotionally misaligned with a more empowered identity. Phrases like *"People like me don't live in houses like that"* are not merely statements—they are fences.

The question then becomes: how do we dismantle these linguistic fences without dishonouring the realities that birthed them? The answer lies not in denial, but in reframing. Instead of saying, *"I'm broke,"* one might say, *"I'm temporarily low on liquid funds, but I'm working on new solutions."* Rather than saying, *"I can't afford it,"* one could ask, *"How can I make this financially sustainable?"* These shifts are not cosmetic. They replace fixed thinking with possibility thinking. They don't erase financial limitation, but they transform it into a navigable challenge rather than an immovable wall.

This reframe must also extend to how we discuss money with others. Social scripting plays a large role in reinforcing poverty consciousness. When peers regularly exchange stories of financial chaos or self-deprecating jokes about overspending, it becomes difficult to speak differently. Those who attempt to adopt more empowered language may be met with suspicion, mockery, or even exclusion. Yet part of evolving one's financial identity is having the courage to speak a different financial language—even if it feels awkward, even if it disrupts group norms.

This courage can be cultivated gradually. Begin by observing your most frequently used financial phrases. Write them down. Examine their emotional tone. Are they expansive or contracting? Empowering or disempowering? Then, consciously craft new phrases that reflect the financial mindset you want to embody. Speak them aloud. Use them in conversation. Write them into your journal or planner. Over time, these new phrases become familiar. They begin to feel true. And once something *feels* true, it becomes far easier to act upon.

This process of linguistic transformation is not about pretending money is easy or ignoring economic challenges. It is about refusing to let disempowering language dictate your financial identity. It is about recognising that words are not neutral—they carry frequency, shape behaviour, and build cognitive architecture. Just as harmful language can keep us small, intentional language can create the scaffolding for financial expansion.

Therapists and coaches working at the intersection of finance and psychology have found that clients who consistently practise mindful language use around money are more likely to follow through on financial plans, recover from setbacks, and take calculated risks. Language, it turns out, is not only reflective of mindset—it is a form of mental wealth. Those who learn to speak with intention begin to think with clarity. And those who think with clarity are better positioned to act with precision.

Ultimately, the choice of financial language is a choice about identity. Do you want to be the person who is always "just getting by," or the person who is building capacity? The person who "can't handle money," or the one who is developing skill and confidence? The person who sees money as the enemy, or the person who sees it as a tool—neutral, flexible, and available to be used in the service of meaningful goals?

Words alone won't change your bank balance. But they *will* change the way you relate to your bank balance. They will change how you interpret financial events, how you respond to challenges, and how you move toward goals. They will shift your posture—from defensive to proactive, from shame to agency, from fear to discernment.

To create wealth, speak as though wealth is already within you—not in denial of reality, but in devotion to potential. Because in the economy of thought, language is currency. Spend it wisely.

The Energetics of Abundance Talk

There is a subtle but profound power in the words we choose—not just in how they shape our thoughts, but in how they condition our energetic presence. The language we use to talk about money does more than reflect a mindset; it projects a vibrational frequency that influences our behaviour, our relationships, and even the opportunities we attract or repel. This is where the disciplines of psychology and metaphysics converge—at the crossroads of language, cognition, and the subtle energies that govern human interaction. "Abundance talk" is not just positive language. It is a deliberate, embodied shift in how we speak, think, and feel about money, grounded in both the neuroscience of behaviour and the metaphysical principle that energy precedes form.

To understand the energetics of abundance talk, we must begin by acknowledging a foundational principle of human psychology: our internal states influence our external realities. This is not mysticism—it is supported by research in affective neuroscience, which shows that emotional states such as gratitude, hopefulness, and curiosity increase neural flexibility, improve problem-solving, and enhance risk tolerance. When you speak from a place of abundance—even if your financial reality is not yet where you want it to be—you are activating the brain's capacity for resilience and expansion. Conversely, language steeped in scarcity, shame, or defeat narrows focus, limits creativity, and reinforces a reactive posture to life.

The metaphysical dimension of abundance talk takes this a step further. Drawing from traditions such as Hermetic philosophy, quantum thought, and Eastern spiritual teachings, the idea is that language emits frequency. Words, when charged with intention and emotion, radiate energetic signatures that ripple outward. Whether one believes in vibrational fields or not, this principle often plays out experientially. Consider how you respond to someone who says, "I'm doing what I can with what I've got—it's working for me so far," versus someone who sighs, "Nothing ever works out for me, no matter what I try." Even if the material facts are similar, the energetic effect is different. One invites collaboration, the other closes the door.

This is not about denying difficulty or pretending abundance into existence. It is about speaking truth from a different state of being—one that aligns with growth, possibility, and internal authority rather than helplessness or lack. Abundance talk, then, is not superficial optimism. It is a form of self-leadership.

Take the case of Alicia, a consultant who began noticing that every time she spoke about her business, she used the phrase, "I'm just trying to survive out here." Though said with humour, the language reflected a deeper belief that she was constantly on the edge of collapse. That belief was shaping her posture in meetings, the way she positioned her services, and even the types of clients she attracted—those who undervalued or exploited her time. With the help of a coach, Alicia shifted her language to: "I'm building something valuable, and I'm learning how to serve at a higher level." The immediate effect was not just internal—it was behavioural. She began raising her rates, setting clearer boundaries, and choosing projects that aligned with her strengths. Her income doubled within six months. The energetic shift preceded the material one.

This principle also applies in more everyday contexts. Someone who constantly says, "I'll never get ahead," is subtly instructing their subconscious to expect limitation. Every opportunity is filtered through a lens of unworthiness or futility. In contrast, someone who says, "I'm exploring new ways to grow," even amid challenge, positions themselves as a creative agent. Their language reinforces their potential rather than their pain. They are not denying struggle—they are choosing the direction of their focus.

From a behavioural standpoint, abundance talk also rewires the feedback loop between language and action. When we speak as if we have agency, we are more likely to take actions that reflect that belief. This is rooted in the psychological concept of *self-efficacy*, developed by Albert Bandura, which refers to a person's belief in their ability to influence outcomes. High self-efficacy correlates with increased motivation, persistence, and adaptability—all of which are essential for financial growth. Language is one of the most immediate and accessible ways to build it.

It is important to note, however, that abundance talk must be anchored in authenticity. Hollow affirmations—words repeated without resonance or emotional integrity—can backfire. If a person says, "I am wealthy beyond measure," while feeling desperate and disconnected, the dissonance may reinforce the opposite belief. What matters is alignment. A more effective starting point might be, "I am learning to build wealth in a way that supports my values." This honours the present reality while leaning into possibility.

Abundance talk also has relational consequences. When we shift the way we speak about money, we shift the energy we bring into conversations with partners, children, clients, and communities. A parent who speaks about budgeting not with dread but with clarity and vision models a different relationship with money. A business leader who discusses investment not as a risk to be feared but as a tool for strategic expansion creates a different field of engagement. The language we use becomes the environment we inhabit—and invite others into.

Metaphysical traditions offer additional insight into this dynamic. The Law of Vibration, often cited in both esoteric and practical circles, suggests that everything in the universe moves and resonates at a frequency, including thought and speech. High-frequency language—characterised by gratitude, vision, and empowerment—is believed to harmonise with high-frequency outcomes. Whether or not one subscribes to this view metaphysically, it has clear psychological and behavioural correlates. Grateful people tend to report better financial outcomes—not because they ignore problems, but because their emotional state supports proactive behaviour, creative thinking, and social cohesion.

This is where abundance talk becomes a tool for personal and cultural change. It invites us to examine the linguistic habits we've inherited from families, communities, or media, and to ask: *Do these words support who I am becoming?* If not, they can be rewritten. This is not just a semantic exercise. It is a form of energetic hygiene. Just as we detox our diets or declutter our homes, we can purify our language to better reflect our aspirations and values.

One practical method is to perform a language audit. Over the course of a week, note the recurring phrases you use about money, especially in moments of stress. Do you use diminishing language? Do you frame desires in terms of impossibility? Are you echoing old narratives that no longer reflect your truth? Once identified, these phrases can be gently replaced with alternatives that retain honesty but shift energy. *"This is a challenge"* can become *"This is an opportunity to grow."* *"I can't afford that"* can evolve into *"I'm not prioritising that right now."* Each adjustment is a recalibration of focus, agency, and emotional tone.

These shifts, while subtle, are cumulative. Just as compound interest builds wealth over time, consistent use of empowered, aligned language builds mental wealth—a reservoir of self-trust, clarity, and emotional sovereignty. This is the essence of abundance: not merely having more, but *feeling whole* regardless of circumstance. And it begins, always, with the words we choose to speak.

In the final analysis, abundance talk is not about pretending everything is fine. It is about choosing to narrate your life from the perspective of creative power, emotional regulation, and conscious alignment. It is about using language as a tool—not just for expression, but for expansion. And when spoken with intention, integrity, and openness, those words do more than inspire—they initiate transformation. They become a current that moves thought into form, and form into fulfilment.

Upgrading Your Financial Vocabulary

The language we use to describe our financial lives is not a passive reflection of reality—it is a powerful architect of it. Words act as cognitive tools, shaping how we perceive ourselves, how we respond to opportunity or adversity, and how we engage with the world of money at both conscious and subconscious levels. When that language is disempowering, it quietly reinforces a narrative of limitation. When it is intentional, constructive, and grounded in self-leadership, it becomes the scaffolding for financial growth. The concept of upgrading your financial vocabulary is not a superficial linguistic exercise. It is a deeply psychological and behavioural intervention that has the power to rewire mindset, behaviour, and outcomes.

Disempowering financial language often sounds casual, even harmless. Phrases like *"I can't afford this," "I'm not good with money," "I'll always be in debt,"* or *"That's just the way things are"* are uttered without much thought. Yet they encode fixed beliefs—beliefs that silently dictate action. Behavioural psychology confirms this: our self-concept is shaped in part by the language we internalise and repeat. When the script is one of helplessness, inadequacy, or resignation, our financial behaviour tends to mirror it. We delay decisions, avoid planning, and resist wealth-building strategies—not necessarily due to lack of information, but because the identity we've verbalised doesn't support those actions.

To reframe this dynamic, we must first acknowledge that every word choice reflects an underlying worldview. Saying *"I can't afford this"* shuts down inquiry and exploration. It positions us as passive recipients of economic circumstances. By contrast, saying *"How can I afford this wisely?"* keeps the door open. It shifts us from resignation to resourcefulness, activating the brain's problem-solving circuitry. This subtle linguistic pivot matters—not only because it changes the tone of self-talk, but because it invites a different behavioural response.

A compelling example of this comes from the coaching practice of Linda Zhang, a financial therapist who works with early-career professionals. One of her clients, Tara, frequently said, *"I'm terrible with money."* Despite being employed, Tara avoided looking at her bank statements and frequently defaulted to overdraft charges. Linda encouraged her to replace this phrase with *"I'm in the process of understanding my finances better."* This new language allowed Tara to approach her money without shame and created a psychological safety zone for learning. Within three months, Tara was not only tracking her expenses but had opened an investment account—something she had previously considered beyond her capabilities.

This is the power of "empowered language"—phrasing that affirms agency, reinforces learning, and encourages intentionality. It doesn't require pretending that challenges don't exist. Rather, it acknowledges them from a position of curiosity and competence. For example, instead of saying, *"I'm stuck in this job,"* one might say, *"I'm exploring how to transition into more aligned work."* Instead of *"I'm drowning in debt,"* a reframe might be, *"I'm actively creating a strategy to reduce what I owe."* The difference is not semantic—it is strategic. It shifts your internal posture and opens up cognitive bandwidth for solutions.

Linguistic psychology supports this view. The words we speak activate corresponding neural pathways. Repetitive negative language, particularly when emotionally charged, strengthens neural circuits associated with stress and avoidance. In contrast, reframed and constructive language activates areas of the brain responsible for planning, empathy, and creative problem-solving. This is not positive thinking in the simplistic sense—it is neuro-linguistic reconditioning. The science is clear: language patterns create thought patterns, which drive behavioural patterns.

Financial education rarely addresses this. Budgets, spreadsheets, and compound interest are taught, but the invisible script—the one that determines whether someone actually implements what they know—is often ignored. And yet, the language we use is what determines whether we see financial tools as empowering resources or intimidating threats. For example, a person might say, *"Investing is too risky for someone like me."* The upgraded version might be, *"I'm learning about investment options that match my comfort level and goals."* This doesn't deny risk—it contextualises it within the scope of personal agency.

In this light, upgrading your financial vocabulary becomes an act of emotional regulation. It helps mitigate the shame, anxiety, and paralysis that often accompany money management, especially for those with histories of financial trauma or cultural scripts of scarcity. Replacing *"I always mess up my finances"* with *"I'm practising more mindful financial habits"* can disarm self-criticism and build self-trust. Over time, this shift alters your baseline orientation to money—from avoidance to engagement, from fear to discernment.

This practice is particularly powerful when integrated into daily routines. For instance, instead of saying, *"I need to cut back,"* one might say, *"I'm choosing to prioritise what matters most."* Instead of saying, *"I can't make ends meet,"* one could say, *"I'm working on strategies to expand my income and reduce unnecessary outflow."* The replacement phrases do not sugar-coat reality—they create a different relational dynamic with it. One where the speaker remains at the centre of decision-making, rather than at the mercy of external conditions.

The implications extend beyond the individual. When empowered financial language is modelled in relationships, families, and workplaces, it reshapes collective norms. A parent who says to a child, *"Let's find a way to make this goal manageable,"* instead of *"We can't afford that—don't ask again,"* teaches both agency and respect. A leader who tells a team, *"We're stewarding our resources carefully to ensure long-term sustainability,"* instead of, *"Budgets are tight, so don't expect much,"* fosters morale while maintaining fiscal responsibility. In both cases, the language used frames money not as a constraint, but as a tool requiring discernment and shared vision.

One useful technique for embedding this shift is to create a personal "language audit"—a two-column journal exercise where you write down commonly used disempowering phrases and then craft their empowered counterparts. This chart becomes a living document—a reference for moments when old scripts surface. Over time, you'll begin to catch yourself in real-time, replacing limiting language with language that supports your goals. It's not about never feeling doubt or anxiety. It's about giving your better self—the one aligned with growth and integrity—a clearer voice.

The real gift of upgrading your financial vocabulary is that it brings you into conversation with your future self—the one who manages money with clarity, communicates needs with confidence, and makes decisions that reflect values rather than fear. That future self doesn't emerge overnight. But with every phrase you refine, you are training your nervous system to trust that growth is possible. You are reauthoring the inner script. And over time, the script becomes belief. Belief becomes behaviour. And behaviour becomes wealth—not just in material terms, but in the form of ease, alignment, and autonomy.

In this respect, language is not only descriptive—it is generative. It constructs the emotional, psychological, and behavioural framework through which we relate to our financial lives. To upgrade your vocabulary, then, is to upgrade your vision. And that vision, made visible through words, becomes the first building block of lasting wealth.

Money Journaling and Wealth Scripts

Every financial decision we make is tethered to a story—one we've often been telling ourselves for years, perhaps decades. These inner narratives, or *wealth scripts*, operate like background code, silently shaping how we think, feel, and act around money. They are rarely scrutinised but always active. Some scripts are empowering, encouraging thoughtful risk-taking and abundance-oriented thinking. Others are quietly corrosive, laced with scarcity, shame, or learned helplessness. Left unchecked, these stories can become self-fulfilling prophecies. Yet when brought into the light, examined with care, and rewritten with intention, they become powerful tools of transformation.

Money journaling is the practice of making the invisible script visible. By putting pen to paper, we engage the mind, body, and emotion in dialogue. This isn't accounting—this is storytelling with purpose. The act of journaling invites clarity; it slows down reactive thoughts, invites reflective inquiry, and makes room for more nuanced perspectives. Unlike budgeting tools or financial trackers that focus on external metrics, money journaling brings attention to *why* we spend, save, or avoid. It is not merely an emotional outlet—it is a strategic reprogramming device.

At its best, money journaling operates at the intersection of cognitive behavioural psychology and expressive writing. Research from psychologists such as Dr James Pennebaker has demonstrated that expressive writing—especially about emotionally charged topics—can reduce stress, improve decision-making, and reframe personal narratives. When applied to financial patterns, journaling becomes a method of cognitive restructuring. It allows us to identify irrational beliefs, challenge automatic thoughts, and embed healthier cognitive frameworks through repeated, conscious articulation.

A central concept in this process is that of *the wealth script*—a deeply ingrained narrative about money, often formed in childhood or shaped by culture, community, and past experience. These scripts might include: *"I have to work twice as hard to make ends meet," "Money always slips away," "I'm not cut out for wealth,"* or *"It's selfish to want more."* While these statements may feel true, they are not immutable facts. They are stories that reflect previous contexts. The work of journaling is to uncover them, examine their origins, and decide whether they still deserve a place in the present.

Take the case of Emeka, a software engineer who grew up in a household where money was discussed only in whispers and often with anxiety. Despite earning a strong income, he struggled with guilt around spending and anxiety about investing. Through journaling, Emeka began writing about his earliest memories of money. He recalled overhearing his parents argue about medical bills and watching his mother forgo basic comforts to prioritise his education. His script had become: *"Spending on myself is selfish."* By bringing this narrative into awareness, Emeka could acknowledge its origin without allowing it to govern his adult life. He rewrote his script to: *"I honour my parents' sacrifices by using money wisely—including for my own well-being."* This reframed perspective allowed him to set financial goals with less guilt and more confidence.

The process of rewriting wealth scripts often begins with targeted prompts—open-ended questions that invite introspection. For example, *What messages did I receive about money growing up?* or *What emotions arise when I look at my bank balance?* These prompts are not meant to extract data, but to evoke emotional truths. They surface the hidden agreements we've made with ourselves—some empowering, others limiting—and provide a platform for conscious revision.

Another powerful prompt is: *If money were a person, what would our relationship be like?* This metaphor often reveals surprising insights. Some describe money as elusive or judgmental. Others see it as a partner they've ignored or a parent they fear disappointing. These metaphors are not to be taken literally, but they help externalise internal conflicts, making them easier to address. Once the relationship has been articulated, new scripts can be written with intentionality: *"Money is a tool I'm learning to use wisely," "Money flows to me when I align with purpose,"* or *"I can trust myself to make financial decisions."*

Visualisation is a complementary technique that enhances the power of journaling. By imagining future scenarios in which money is handled with calm, clarity, and competence, the brain begins to create new neural templates. Neuroscientific research shows that the brain does not distinguish strongly between vividly imagined experiences and real ones—repeated visualisation can, over time, make new behaviours feel more natural. When paired with journaling, visualisation helps bridge the gap between current identity and aspirational identity. Writing about future success as though it were already unfolding—*"I review my finances with confidence and curiosity each week"*—builds emotional familiarity with the desired state.

The integration of journaling and visualisation is particularly effective in breaking patterns of financial avoidance. Avoidance is a common symptom of money-related stress and often stems from fear of confronting discomfort—be it debt, overspending, or the unknown. Journaling offers a way to face that discomfort incrementally, in a space of safety and non-judgement. It gives structure to emotional chaos. Rather than spiralling into shame or paralysis, the individual gains a structured outlet for exploration. Over time, this builds what psychologists call *affect tolerance*—the ability to stay present with uncomfortable emotions without being overwhelmed.

This practice also reorients us toward intentionality. When journaling is used not only to process the past but to articulate the future, it becomes a tool of authorship. Each entry becomes an act of design: the deliberate shaping of a financial identity rooted in values, integrity, and self-trust. This is crucial because most people don't set out to create a dysfunctional relationship with money—it's simply inherited, absorbed, or unconsciously repeated. Money journaling interrupts that inertia. It says, in effect: *I get to choose what money means to me.*

For example, Priya, a freelancer with inconsistent income, began a weekly journaling ritual in which she reviewed her finances alongside the question: *What did I learn about myself through money this week?* Sometimes the answer was practical—"I overspent when I didn't plan meals." Other times it was emotional—"I avoided invoicing because I was afraid of rejection." Over months, these insights formed the foundation of new scripts, such as: *"My income is a reflection of my clarity and boundaries."* Her financial habits improved not through restriction, but through reflection.

Critically, journaling should not be seen as a silver bullet. It is not a substitute for financial education or professional advice. But it *does* amplify the effectiveness of those tools by aligning your inner landscape with your outer actions. When the stories we tell ourselves support our goals rather than sabotage them, every financial task becomes more navigable—from budgeting to investing to negotiating.

Furthermore, money journaling serves as a lifelong practice rather than a one-time fix. Our financial lives evolve, and so do the scripts we carry. What served us in our twenties may no longer fit in our forties. What was once protective may now be restrictive. Journaling provides an ongoing space to update those narratives, to renegotiate what wealth means, and to remain conscious authors of our economic lives.

Ultimately, money journaling is not about producing perfect prose or arriving at tidy conclusions. It is about cultivating a habit of introspection and authorship. It is about speaking to yourself on the page with honesty and curiosity, rewriting what no longer serves, and rehearsing the future you are building—one word, one belief, one script at a time. In a world that often treats wealth as merely numerical, this practice reclaims it as narrative. And when that narrative is aligned, wealth becomes not just what we have, but how we live.

Speaking Your New Financial Identity

The words we use to describe ourselves shape how others see us—and even more importantly, how we see ourselves. This is especially true when it comes to money. Financial identity is not just about what you earn, spend, or save. It's about how you *speak* about those actions and the beliefs they signal. The process of reprogramming limiting beliefs around money must eventually translate into public expression. When you begin to speak differently about money—with partners, friends, clients, or colleagues—you reinforce your new mindset and invite your environment to align with it. This is where personal transformation becomes relational, and private conviction evolves into public embodiment.

Financial self-talk is one thing; financial self-expression is another. The former happens in solitude, through journaling, reflection, or internal dialogue. The latter unfolds in the presence of others, and it tests the strength of your new script against old social patterns. For many, this stage can feel vulnerable. Saying *"I'm prioritising long-term wealth building,"* or *"I'm charging more for my work,"* or *"I'm focusing on financial boundaries,"* may meet resistance or misunderstanding. But it is precisely in these conversations that your financial identity solidifies—not by consensus, but by conscious reinforcement.

Speaking your new financial identity begins with clarity. You must know what you now believe about money and who you are becoming financially. This clarity cannot be outsourced. It emerges from deep inner work—recognising old scripts, replacing them with empowered beliefs, and practicing new behaviours until they begin to feel congruent. Without this internal coherence, your words will lack authenticity, and others will sense the incongruity. But when your language reflects a truth you are actively living, it becomes magnetic. It commands attention not through volume, but through resonance.

This internal-external alignment is crucial in intimate partnerships. Money is a leading source of stress in relationships not just because of differing values, but because of differing vocabularies. One partner might say *"We need to be more responsible,"* while the other hears *"You're irresponsible."* A shift in tone, language, and framing can make all the difference. Speaking from your new financial identity doesn't mean dominating the conversation; it means using language that is clear, non-reactive, and reflective of the growth you've committed to.

For example, instead of saying, *"You spend too much,"* a person aligned with their new identity might say, *"I'm working on aligning my spending with long-term goals, and I'd love for us to explore that together."* This subtle reframe reduces defensiveness and centres the conversation around shared values rather than personal shortcomings. It models responsibility without blame. And it makes the new financial self—a person who is values-driven, conscious, and empowered—visible in the dialogue.

This kind of language also becomes important in friendships. Many people find themselves trapped in spending habits or financial roles that no longer serve them simply because their social group reinforces an outdated identity. Perhaps you were always "the generous one," always paying the bill or saying yes to costly outings. Or maybe you've been the friend who downplayed your success to maintain comfort or avoid envy. Speaking your new financial identity might mean saying, *"I'm focusing on intentional spending right now, so I'll pass on the weekend trip,"* or *"I've started paying more attention to how I price my time and energy."* These statements are not explanations to justify change—they are declarations that set a new tone.

Such declarations require emotional intelligence. They must be delivered with conviction but without superiority. The goal is not to signal virtue or status, but to reflect alignment. Your new financial language should not alienate—it should invite. When friends hear you speak about money with grounded confidence and clarity, it may challenge their own scripts—but it also gives them permission to explore their own. You become a model of possibility, not just for your financial success, but for financial honesty.

In professional contexts, the way you speak about money can dramatically influence outcomes. Whether you're negotiating fees, discussing budgets, or leading a team, your financial language signals how you perceive value—yours and others'. Professionals who speak with hesitation around pricing, for instance, often inadvertently signal lack of confidence. Replacing *"If that's too much, I understand"* with *"This reflects the value and results I bring"* sends a radically different message. One invites bargaining. The other affirms worth.

Consider Rohan, a creative consultant who habitually underpriced his services because he feared rejection. After revising his financial beliefs, he began using language that reflected his new sense of value: *"This fee includes not just deliverables but strategic insight and time-tested experience."* He also practised saying, *"I'm confident this is a fair rate, and I'm happy to answer any questions about how I arrived at it."* The effect was immediate. Clients respected his boundaries, negotiation became collaborative rather than defensive, and his income increased—without having to 'hustle harder.'

The shift in language also extended to how Rohan spoke to himself. Before, he'd say, *"I hope they think I'm worth it."* Now, he says, *"I choose clients who value what I offer."* The change in phrasing reflects a change in posture—from hope to discernment, from approval-seeking to alignment. This self-possession is the essence of a spoken financial identity: you're no longer asking others to define your worth. You're articulating it clearly and letting the right opportunities respond.

It's important to note that this kind of empowered financial language does not emerge from bravado or performance. It arises from a place of embodied conviction. And it's cultivated through practice—first in safe spaces (a journal, a coaching session), then in progressively more complex interactions. It might begin with replacing passive phrases like *"I'm trying to get better with money"* with *"I'm actively building financial systems that support my goals."* Or with replacing the apologetic *"I know it's expensive, but..."* with *"This investment reflects the quality of the outcome."* Over time, these new linguistic habits become natural. They become part of how you *exist* in the world—not just how you talk about it.

This evolution can feel disruptive at first. You may lose approval from those who preferred your older identity—especially if your prior money language was built around sacrifice, silence, or self-erasure. But clarity always comes with a cost. And the cost of not speaking your financial truth is far greater: misaligned relationships, under-earning, chronic resentment, and an internal schism between who you are and who you perform.

Ultimately, speaking your new financial identity is not just about language—it's about leadership. It is about taking responsibility for how you show up in conversations about value, desire, responsibility, and growth. It is about creating coherence between your internal evolution and your external communication. And it is about building a financial life that feels not only prosperous, but authentic—because it is built on words that reflect who you have chosen to become.

So speak as the person you are becoming. Let your words reflect your values. Let your tone embody your clarity. Let your conversations model the alignment you've worked to build. Because when you speak from truth, with compassion and confidence, your world listens—and begins to reflect that truth back.

Chapter 6
Habits That Hardwire Abundance

Abundance, contrary to popular gloss, isn't some airy mindset you simply adopt—it's a discipline. A lived practice. And like any discipline, it's not sculpted by rare epiphanies or grand gestures, but by what we do—reliably, even quietly—day after day. While a breakthrough can light the path, it's the cadence of daily habits that threads wealth into the fibres of one's life. These habits don't require heroic effort. In truth, the most transformative are usually subtle, barely noticeable in isolation. But repeated with care, they gain momentum. Over time, they reshape not only our bank accounts, but our relationship to money itself.

We're often taught to fixate on the mechanics—budgets, investments, multiple income streams. Vital, yes. But these are scaffolds. What tends to get lost in the shuffle is the deeper architecture—the behavioural spine that makes such strategies sustainable. Because without consistent habits grounded in a strong sense of self, even the cleverest plan buckles under the weight of fatigue, indecision, or apathy. Habits, in this light, function less as routines and more as quiet rituals—daily acts that reinforce not just what we do, but who we believe ourselves to be.

Think of your mornings and evenings as bookends for identity. How you begin and end the day subtly sculpts your sense of agency and abundance. When you fold financial mindfulness into these transitions—perhaps through gratitude journaling, visualising your financial future, or a brief moment of reflective stillness—you start to condition your nervous system. You're teaching it that money is not danger, not chaos, not shame. But something navigable. Something safe. Even jotting down a modest success like "Paid my electricity bill on time" tilts the mental lens from scarcity to progress. These aren't tricks of positive thinking. They are groundwork. Neural and emotional.

There's science here, too. Behavioural research reminds us that not all habits are equal. The 80/20 rule—that curious truth that a small portion of our actions yield the lion's share of results—applies just as strongly to money. Some habits matter disproportionately. Take expense tracking. Done with neutrality (not judgment), it provides data that clarifies. Or consider automation—diverting a set percentage of income into savings or investments. It removes the variable of willpower entirely. These are what might be called keystone habits: modest in effort, high in yield. They run in the background, quietly accruing results.

To build such habits without burning out, there's a trick: link the new to the familiar. Behavioural experts—James Clear among them—call it "habit stacking." The principle is straightforward: attach a new practice to an existing routine. You're not reinventing your life; you're folding something new into the rhythm you already have. Review your weekly spending while your coffee brews. Journal about money while brushing your teeth. In doing so, you shift the perception: money habits are no longer chores. They're simply part of life's fabric.

Why does this matter? Because decision fatigue is insidious. Each day, we're ambushed by choices—from the mundane to the meaningful—and every one chips away at our cognitive reserves. The more taxing a financial habit is, the more fragile it becomes. This is why streamlined systems often beat discipline. Automate your bills. Set recurring calendar nudges for financial check-ins. Use budgeting tools that remove the clutter and friction. When systems do the heavy lifting, good behaviour becomes the path of least resistance.

Leon, a freelance designer, offers a case in point. Earning well, yet saving little, his problem wasn't income—it was inertia. By the time he remembered to transfer money into savings, he was mentally spent. A coach helped him set up an automatic 10% transfer after each client payment. Decision removed, savings climbed. Six months later, he'd set aside more than he had in the past two years combined. The genius of it? Nothing flashy. He simply built around his limits instead of trying to will his way past them.

But let's not forget—efficiency isn't everything. There's also the question of enjoyment. Financial habits that feel like punishment rarely stick. Neuroscience supports this: behaviours linked to pleasure are far more likely to recur. Enter gamification. Turn savings goals into a visual ladder. Use points or colour-coded charts to track milestones. It's not about trivialising money. It's about making the process feel like movement, not drudgery.

Gamification, when done right, doesn't cheapen discipline—it personalises it. It invites engagement from the part of the brain that craves reward. Suddenly, saving doesn't mean deprivation; it signals progress. Budgeting stops being an act of scarcity and becomes one of structure, even empowerment. Particularly for those who've struggled with consistency, this emotional pivot can be the difference between another failed attempt and a sustainable shift.

And yet, none of this holds without anchoring. Habits must flow from identity, or they wither. Behaviour theorist B.J. Fogg has long argued that lasting change roots itself in self-concept. If you see yourself as "financially grounded," then updating your budget isn't a burden—it's congruent. If you adopt the identity of "someone building intergenerational wealth," then passing on impulse buys isn't deprivation—it's clarity. These habits become mirrors, reflecting and reinforcing who you believe yourself to be.

This is especially potent when confronting inherited financial beliefs. Many of us are the carriers of hand-me-down money stories: that wealth must be hoarded, that spending is shameful, or that success comes with moral compromise. Repeating abundance-oriented habits—ones that suggest sufficiency, balance, intention—helps disrupt those narratives. Not just intellectually, but somatically. The nervous system learns a new script. Instead of defaulting to vigilance or guilt, it begins to associate money with stability, even grace.

None of this, it must be said, requires perfection. In fact, the pursuit of perfection is often what derails us. The goal isn't pristine execution, but resilient consistency. Miss a day? Fine. That's not failure—it's information. A signal to tweak the structure, not abandon the mission. Journaling fell off? Ask why. Was the timing wrong? The setting off? Habits, at their best, are adaptive tools—not measuring sticks for moral worth.

As these behaviours become woven into your daily rhythm, something subtle yet profound begins to shift. Abundance no longer feels like a distant destination. It becomes tangible. Embodied. You stop striving to be "better with money" and start simply being someone who lives in financial alignment—calm, intentional, structured. Over time, the compounding effect is not just numerical. It's emotional. These habits build confidence. They ease the grip of shame. They create the kind of stability from which vision—real vision—can emerge.

This chapter, then, isn't a productivity sermon. It's a call to design a life in which abundance isn't an occasional guest, but a regular presence. Where your daily behaviours echo your deeper values. Where money is not a source of friction or fear, but a domain of clarity, purpose, and quietly evolving mastery. Not through force. Not through luck. But through the quiet power of repetition—ritual by ritual, habit by habit, choice by deliberate choice.

Daily Wealth Rituals: Morning and Evening Routines to Anchor the New Mindset

Wealth is more than the accumulation of assets; it is a psychological orientation, a way of perceiving and interacting with the world. At the core of sustainable financial growth is not just knowledge or opportunity, but rhythm—the daily cadence of behaviours and rituals that reinforce a sense of abundance, clarity, and agency. Morning and evening routines, often overlooked in traditional financial planning, hold transformative potential for anchoring a mindset of prosperity. These rituals, grounded in gratitude, micro-journaling, and visualisation, serve not only to orient behaviour but to regulate the nervous system, sharpen decision-making, and reprogramme internal narratives about money.

The first moments of the day are neurologically and psychologically potent. Upon waking, the brain transitions from theta to alpha to beta wave states—an ideal window for suggestion, reflection, and intention-setting. It is during this phase that the subconscious mind is most receptive to influence. A deliberate morning wealth ritual makes use of this cognitive plasticity to install beliefs and behaviours aligned with financial wellbeing. Rather than reaching for a device or launching into urgency, a few structured minutes of reflection can fundamentally shift the emotional tone of the day.

Gratitude is the cornerstone of any effective wealth ritual. Numerous studies in positive psychology, including those led by Dr Robert Emmons at the University of California, have demonstrated that consistent gratitude practice improves wellbeing, reduces depressive symptoms, and increases resilience. When applied to finance, gratitude tempers the scarcity mindset that many people carry—often unconsciously—into every financial decision. By listing even modest financial gratitudes each morning, such as "I have food in my fridge," "I paid my rent on time," or "I am learning how to manage my resources," individuals reframe their experience of sufficiency. This reframe is not about ignoring economic challenges but about anchoring the emotional nervous system in enoughness, which reduces impulsivity and fosters a capacity for delayed gratification.

Complementing gratitude is micro-journaling—a brief, focused exercise designed to track emotional and behavioural patterns related to money. This is not about balancing accounts or itemising expenses, but about capturing thought-emotion links. A morning prompt might ask: *"What money-related thought did I wake up with today?"* or *"How do I want to show up financially in the next 24 hours?"* These micro-entries—often no more than three to five sentences—build self-awareness over time. They also offer a breadcrumb trail for recognising recurring narratives, whether empowering or limiting. When a person begins to see that they consistently write, *"I feel anxious about checking my bank account,"* they are better equipped to address the belief systems and behavioural avoidance underpinning that emotion.

The third pillar of the morning ritual is visualisation—a technique long embraced by elite athletes, entrepreneurs, and behavioural therapists for its role in priming the brain for goal-oriented action. Visualising oneself engaging in financially empowered behaviour—asking for a raise, investing confidently, saying no to misaligned spending—activates mirror neurons and begins to normalise success at a somatic level. Neuroscientific research indicates that the brain encodes imagined experiences in ways strikingly similar to real ones.

Practised consistently, visualisation does not replace action; it prepares the mind and body to recognise and seize opportunities with less resistance and more clarity.

Evening rituals serve a different but equally critical function. Where morning routines are about intention and priming, evening practices are about integration and closure. The final thirty minutes before sleep are a neurobiologically sensitive period in which the subconscious consolidates the emotional tone of the day. Financial stress left unprocessed at bedtime does not simply fade—it often amplifies overnight, contributing to restless sleep, cortisol spikes, and impaired cognitive function the following day. A brief evening wealth ritual helps metabolise the day's experiences and restore a sense of control.

A practical evening practice might begin with a short reflection on one financial action—however minor—that aligned with one's values. This could be as simple as *"I chose not to buy something impulsively,"* or *"I transferred £20 to my savings account."* Acknowledging this reinforces self-efficacy, the belief that one's actions have meaningful impact. This principle is foundational in behavioural psychology: when people track small wins, they become more consistent in their habits and less reliant on sporadic motivation.

Another useful evening prompt is *"What did I learn today about myself and money?"* This question positions every experience—whether a setback, success, or mundane routine—as data in service of growth. Over time, this builds a learning mindset, which is more resilient and adaptive than a performance-based mindset. Rather than framing a budgeting slip-up as failure, the journaller might write, *"I learned that I tend to overspend when I'm emotionally depleted. I'll plan ahead for nourishment next time."* This subtle reframing reduces shame and increases strategic thinking.

Visualisation also has a role to play at night. Rather than planning or worrying, this is a moment for soft imagining. Envisioning a future where money flows through life in alignment with purpose, generosity, and clarity helps soothe financial anxiety and embeds a subconscious blueprint of abundance. Importantly, this visualisation is not a fantasy about wealth for wealth's sake. It is a sensorial rehearsal of what it feels like to live in harmony with one's values and resources. Done consistently, it reshapes the emotional associations with money—from stress to spaciousness, from reactivity to responsiveness.

Ritualising these practices does not mean rigid adherence. The power lies in their consistency, not their perfection. A five-minute practice done daily is more effective than an elaborate routine done sporadically. The goal is not to perform wealth consciousness but to embody it. That embodiment begins in quiet, often invisible moments: pen on paper before the house stirs, a breath before opening the banking app, a whispered affirmation before switching off the light.

Real-world examples abound. Consider Jamila, a social worker who once viewed money management as a source of shame. Through a morning practice of writing down three financial gratitudes and a short visualisation of herself confidently paying bills and setting financial boundaries, she gradually rewired her emotional relationship with money. Within a year, she had cleared consumer debt and started mentoring others on basic financial literacy—not because of a windfall, but because she began each day from a place of empowered presence.

Or Daniel, a freelance videographer who introduced a bedtime habit of tracking one value-aligned money decision each day. He noticed patterns in his emotional spending and began rerouting that energy into a "vision fund" for future business investments. The act of noticing, reinforcing, and celebrating these decisions transformed his sense of control—and his results followed.

These practices also serve as emotional inoculations against a culture that often equates financial worth with self-worth, and productivity with value. In creating daily rituals, we reclaim money from abstraction and ground it in care, reflection, and meaning. We transform it from a source of fear into a site of practice. And we remind ourselves, day by day, that abundance is not something we arrive at—it is something we *rehearse.*

Ultimately, wealth rituals are not about performance or perfection. They are acts of alignment—subtle, steady, sacred. They give structure to intention and breath to belief. They invite us to live not just with more money, but with more integrity in how we relate to it. In that sense, they do not merely support wealth; they *become* wealth—embodied, practiced, and made real in the quiet moments that shape a life.

The 80/20 of Financial Progress: Focus on the Few High-Impact Habits That Truly Move the Needle

In personal finance, complexity often masquerades as intelligence. The more elaborate the system, the more knowledgeable we assume its creator must be. But in reality, sustainable financial success is seldom about doing *more*—it is about doing *less* with greater precision. This is the essence of the 80/20 principle, also known as the Pareto Principle: a small number of behaviours typically produce the majority of results. Applied to finance, this means that a handful of carefully chosen habits can dramatically alter one's financial trajectory, while countless others—though well-intentioned—deliver marginal returns at best.

Understanding the 80/20 principle in this context demands a shift in thinking. Instead of asking, "What else can I do to improve my financial life?" a more useful question is, "Which few behaviours consistently deliver the most impact—and how can I master them?" This kind of focus not only saves time and energy, but also protects against burnout and decision fatigue, two of the most common culprits behind financial inconsistency. The goal is not perfection across the board, but deliberate excellence in a few key areas.

Tracking money is one of those high-leverage behaviours. Yet it is also one of the most emotionally charged. Many people avoid reviewing their bank statements or budgeting apps not because they lack time or tools, but because the act of looking carries with it the weight of self-judgement. Numbers become evidence not just of transactions, but of identity: "I'm bad with money," "I'm irresponsible," or "I can't be trusted." To make tracking a truly impactful habit, it must be decoupled from shame. This begins by reframing the act not as an audit, but as an act of clarity—akin to stepping on a scale not to criticise, but to calibrate. You cannot change what you do not measure, and you cannot measure what you are afraid to face.

One way to neutralise the emotional charge of tracking is through regular, low-stakes check-ins. For example, instead of a once-monthly reckoning that feels like a courtroom, five-minute weekly reflections can normalise the data and make patterns easier to see. It's not about tracking every penny—it's about gaining awareness of inflows, outflows, and friction points. As clarity increases, so does confidence. And with confidence comes improved decision-making: fewer reactive purchases, more intentional spending, and greater alignment with long-term goals.

Another habit with disproportionate power is automation. In behavioural economics, this is referred to as *choice architecture*—the design of systems that make the desired behaviour the path of least resistance. When savings, investments, or bill payments happen automatically, they no longer rely on willpower, which is finite and inconsistent. Instead, these actions become default behaviours—predictable, repeatable, and emotionally neutral. The result is momentum without mental taxation.

The power of automation lies in its compound effect. Consider the difference between someone who manually transfers money into a savings account "when they remember," versus someone whose system does it the day after each payday. Over a year, the difference in outcomes is staggering—not because one is more intelligent or disciplined, but because one has outsourced the decision to a system. Financial progress becomes less about discipline and more about design.

Real-world examples reinforce this. Take Nia, a teacher in her mid-thirties who had struggled for years to maintain any kind of savings. After several failed attempts at budgeting, she worked with a coach who helped her set up a system where 15 percent of her salary was split automatically across three goals: emergency fund, travel, and long-term investing. Within 18 months, she had more financial security than she'd had in the previous decade. Not because she became more frugal, but because she structured a high-impact habit and let time do the heavy lifting.

Not all habits, however, need to be automated to be effective. Some thrive on consciousness—particularly habits that relate to values alignment. One such habit is periodic reflection on spending satisfaction. Once a week, asking, *"Which expenses brought genuine fulfilment?"* and *"Which ones felt hollow or misaligned?"* allows individuals to recalibrate their financial lives around meaning rather than impulse. Over time, this habit increases what psychologists call *financial intentionality*—the degree to which your money reflects your values. It also reduces the emotional hangover of misaligned spending and enhances long-term satisfaction.

Another deceptively simple but high-impact habit is the regular setting and reviewing of short-term financial targets. While long-term goals like retirement are important, they can feel abstract and distant. In contrast, short-term milestones—such as paying down a credit card, saving for a specific purchase, or hitting a monthly earnings target—offer emotional immediacy. They create a sense of momentum, and when tracked visibly (on a calendar, a journal, or a whiteboard), they turn the abstract into something tactile. The brain responds powerfully to visible progress. Motivation increases. Procrastination diminishes. And confidence compounds.

This principle also applies to debt reduction, a financial behaviour often laced with shame and avoidance. Focusing on one account at a time, tracking the shrinking balance, and celebrating micro-victories can transform the process from drudgery to empowerment. What matters is not the size of the step, but the consistency of its repetition. The cumulative impact is disproportionate to the effort required.

What unites all these high-impact habits is not their complexity, but their clarity. They are simple, strategic, and identity-reinforcing. They don't require you to become someone else—they help you become the most aligned version of who you already are. This is a crucial distinction, because many people fail financially not due to laziness or ignorance, but because they're pursuing strategies that conflict with their natural rhythms, values, or psychological needs. When a habit feels like a mismatch, it creates resistance. But when it feels like an extension of your chosen identity, it becomes frictionless.

Importantly, the 80/20 principle can also be applied to financial *mistakes*. Not all errors are created equal. Some decisions—like consistently overspending on housing, or failing to insure key assets—have far more damaging consequences than sporadic indulgences or forgotten subscriptions. Likewise, some fears—such as avoiding investment entirely due to volatility—can erode long-term wealth more than the occasional market loss. Knowing which few behaviours account for most of your setbacks allows you to correct course strategically, without getting lost in minutiae.

This perspective invites a more compassionate, results-oriented approach to financial self-assessment. Instead of agonising over every transaction or obsessing over minor leaks in the budget, the focus becomes strategic: *What are the few shifts I can make that will dramatically improve my outcomes?* This question not only clarifies priorities—it liberates attention from financial micromanagement and creates space for deeper engagement with life.

Ultimately, the 80/20 of financial progress is about strategic minimalism. It is about trading effort for elegance, and anxiety for alignment. When you identify and commit to a handful of high-leverage habits—tracking money without shame, automating savings, aligning spending with values—you unlock a disproportionate return on effort. Progress accelerates. Confidence rises. And money begins to feel less like a battle and more like a collaboration.

This is not to say that nuance and depth have no place in personal finance. But true sophistication lies not in complexity for its own sake, but in clarity and intentionality. A financially empowered life is not built on doing everything—it is built on doing a few things exceptionally well, consistently, and in alignment with who you are becoming. And that begins with asking, every day: *What truly moves the needle—and am I doing it with care, purpose, and trust?*

Habit Stacking for Financial Consistency: Pairing Wealth-Building Habits with Existing Routines

In the architecture of lasting behavioural change, consistency trumps intensity. It is not the grand gestures or once-a-year resolutions that sculpt a financially empowered life, but the small, daily behaviours performed almost without thought—those that accumulate, compound, and quietly define who we are becoming. For this reason, the method of habit stacking has emerged as one of the most effective tools in the psychology of behaviour change. The concept is simple yet transformative: link a new behaviour you wish to adopt with a well-established habit already embedded in your daily routine. The result is reduced friction, increased consistency, and, crucially, a natural rhythm of wealth-building that feels integrated rather than forced.

The idea of habit stacking gained prominence through the work of behaviour scientist B.J. Fogg and later popularised by James Clear in *Atomic Habits*. The approach leverages a well-known principle in neuroscience: the brain thrives on cues. Habits do not exist in isolation; they are triggered by context—time of day, location, emotional state, or preceding action. When a new habit is anchored to an existing behaviour, the cognitive effort required to initiate it diminishes significantly. Instead of relying on willpower or motivation—both notoriously unreliable—we rely on the reliability of routine. This principle is particularly potent when applied to financial habits, which often evoke resistance, avoidance, or emotional fatigue.

Financial behaviours, especially those related to tracking, planning, or reflecting, are often postponed not because of complexity, but because they lack a natural entry point. People know they "should" budget, review expenses, or set goals, but these actions float in conceptual space, detached from the structure of daily life. Habit stacking brings them down to earth. Reviewing your weekly spending becomes part of your Sunday evening tea ritual. Checking your savings goals aligns with your mid-morning coffee. Updating your financial journal happens just after brushing your teeth at night. These pairings are not random—they are intentional integrations designed to make finance feel as regular and unremarkable as brushing one's teeth.

Take, for example, the case of Harpreet, a small business owner who struggled to track expenses consistently. The act itself took less than five minutes, yet he found himself skipping it for weeks. After exploring his routines, he decided to pair expense tracking with something he did without fail: plugging in his laptop at the end of the workday. Now, when he connected the charger, it became the cue to open his finance app, review his transactions, and log expenses. Within weeks, the habit was automatic—not because he had more discipline, but because he had designed the behaviour to run on momentum, not memory.

The brilliance of habit stacking lies in its subtlety. Financial consistency becomes the by-product of systems design, not constant effort. This aligns with what behavioural economists call *bounded rationality*—the understanding that humans operate within cognitive limits and must conserve mental energy for higher-order decisions. By reducing the need to decide *when*, *how*, or *whether* to perform a financial habit, habit stacking makes the habit itself more sustainable.

The technique also mitigates a common psychological barrier: perceived effort. Many people avoid money-related tasks because they seem daunting or emotionally taxing. But when a task is linked to a neutral or pleasurable routine, the emotional load decreases. Imagine pairing financial visualisation with your morning meditation or a budgeting review with a favourite podcast. The positive association enhances compliance. Over time, the task becomes part of a familiar pattern, no longer requiring emotional negotiation.

This is not merely behavioural theory—it is supported by empirical research. Studies in habit formation, including those conducted at University College London, have found that the strongest predictor of habit maintenance is context stability—the consistency of time, place, and preceding behaviour. The more predictable the cue, the more automatic the behaviour becomes. For financial habits, which often battle against old scripts of avoidance or shame, this contextual anchoring is critical. It shifts the dynamic from reactive to proactive, from episodic to rhythmic.

Consider the example of Natalie, a freelance designer navigating variable income. Budgeting felt irrelevant during lean months and redundant during flush ones. Her coach encouraged her to establish a daily wealth ritual tied to an existing habit: morning coffee. Each day, before taking her first sip, she would spend two minutes updating a micro-journal noting inflow, outflow, and emotional tone. This practice not only improved her awareness—it helped her build a relationship with money that felt stable, regardless of cash flow. The anchoring of the habit to her beloved morning ritual gave the behaviour both structure and emotional resonance.

This emotional component cannot be overstated. Many financial habits fail not because of design flaws but because of emotional resistance—guilt, fear, overwhelm. Habit stacking bypasses these emotional roadblocks by embedding the new behaviour within a framework of familiarity. Over time, what once felt effortful becomes embodied. The new habit is not something you *do*—it becomes part of who you *are*. You are the person who reflects on spending while winding down for the night. You are the person who sets financial intentions while packing lunch. These micro-identities solidify through repetition, anchoring a broader self-concept of financial agency and responsibility.

The technique is also scalable. A beginner might start with one habit stack—perhaps reviewing spending every Friday after logging off from work. As confidence grows, more stacks can be added: goal-setting on the first of the month with morning journaling, income tracking after invoicing, or net worth reviews every quarter aligned with calendar planning. The key is not volume but alignment. Each new habit should be tied to a routine that is already stable and emotionally neutral or positive. The pairing ensures that the financial behaviour piggybacks on the consistency and emotional ease of the existing one.

Habit stacking also dovetails elegantly with identity-based habit formation. According to research from Stanford's Behaviour Design Lab, habits that reinforce a desired identity are more likely to persist. When financial actions are stacked onto routines that already reflect self-care, productivity, or responsibility, the identity reinforcement is multiplied. It's no longer just about reviewing a budget—it's about being the kind of person who is organised, intentional, and values alignment.

Importantly, habit stacking doesn't require the perfect conditions to begin. It thrives on imperfection and iteration. The first version of a stack may feel awkward or misaligned. But with reflection and refinement, the pairings become seamless. Over time, they become the invisible architecture of financial wellness—low in effort, high in return.

The practice also resists the all-or-nothing mindset that derails so many attempts at behavioural change. If a stack is missed one day, it does not derail the system. The stability of the cue ensures that the habit has another chance to be enacted the next day. This resilience is key. Consistency is not the absence of failure—it is the capacity to return to the pattern without punishment or shame.

Ultimately, habit stacking is not about doing more—it is about doing *better*. It is about weaving financial intention into the fabric of daily life, not as an afterthought, but as an integrated rhythm. It transforms wealth-building from a sporadic ambition into a lived experience, grounded in systems, psychology, and self-awareness. In this way, financial consistency becomes not a goal, but a practice—anchored in everyday actions, repeated with ease, and aligned with the life you are consciously choosing to build.

Friction-Free Systems Over Willpower: Designing for Effortless Financial Progress

If there is one lesson that modern behavioural science has delivered with unwavering consistency, it is this: willpower is a weak and unreliable force for long-term behavioural change. We tend to overestimate our capacity to make disciplined financial decisions day after day, believing that if we simply try harder, we will save more, spend less, and finally master our money. Yet decades of research into decision-making, cognitive overload, and habit formation suggest the opposite. The most consistent, financially empowered individuals are not those with Herculean self-control—they are those who have engineered their environments to make desired behaviours automatic. They design friction-free systems that remove decision-making from the equation, replacing reliance on motivation with the stability of structure.

At the core of this philosophy is the understanding that financial choices, like all decisions, are subject to a phenomenon known as decision fatigue. Every day, we make hundreds of micro-decisions—from what to eat for breakfast to how to respond to emails. Each choice draws on a finite reservoir of mental energy. As that energy depletes, our capacity to make wise decisions—especially those requiring long-term thinking, like saving or investing—diminishes sharply. In this depleted state, we become more prone to impulse spending, avoidance of financial tasks, and emotional reactions to money stressors.

The antidote to this fatigue is not more discipline. It is automation. When key financial behaviours are set to run on autopilot, they no longer compete for cognitive resources. Instead of deciding every month whether to move money into a savings account, for example, an automated transfer makes the decision once—and lets the system execute it indefinitely. This shift is subtle in action but profound in impact. It transforms a fragile intention into a stable process.

Consider the case of Leah, a freelance illustrator who often found herself scrambling to save money at the end of each month. Despite good intentions, the unpredictability of her income and the variability of her expenses made manual saving difficult. After working with a financial coach, she set up an automated system that transferred a percentage of every client payment to a high-yield savings account. The key innovation was tying the transfer not to a fixed calendar date, but to the arrival of income—a move that matched her financial reality. Within six months, Leah had built an emergency fund that had previously felt unattainable. Her behaviour had not become more disciplined—her system had become smarter.

Beyond automated transfers, friction-free financial systems include minimalist budgeting tools that streamline decision-making. Traditional budgeting, while intellectually sound, often falters in practice due to its complexity and rigidity. In contrast, minimalist budgeting frameworks—such as the "80/20 approach" or "bucket budgeting"—focus on a few key spending categories and flexible guidelines rather than exhaustive line items. These tools reduce friction by removing the burden of constant categorisation and recalibration. They offer a bird's-eye view of spending without the tedium of micro-tracking, allowing users to stay engaged without becoming overwhelmed.

Apps like You Need a Budget (YNAB), Emma, or Plum illustrate how digital design can reduce behavioural friction. They provide visual cues, real-time notifications, and simplified dashboards that help users stay oriented without requiring significant cognitive input. The principle at work here is known as *choice architecture*: the design of an environment in which decisions are made. When a budgeting app defaults to saving before spending, or when it nudges the user to reflect before a large purchase, it is not controlling the user—it is supporting the user's higher-order goals with well-timed prompts. These digital nudges are informed by research in behavioural economics, including the seminal work of Richard Thaler and Cass Sunstein, who argued that small design features can radically shift outcomes without removing autonomy.

The most effective friction-free systems are those that remove temptation, eliminate ambiguity, and reduce the number of financial decisions required per day. For instance, setting up a separate account for recurring bills and routing fixed expenses through it ensures that essentials are always covered, reducing anxiety and decision clutter. Similarly, using browser extensions that block retail sites or disable one-click purchases can shield the mind from impulse triggers in moments of fatigue. These are not signs of weakness—they are signs of intelligent design.

It is worth noting that removing friction is not the same as removing effort altogether. Rather, it is about reallocating effort to where it matters most. When the system handles routine tasks—saving, paying bills, allocating spending categories—your energy is freed to focus on strategic thinking: how to grow income, how to invest wisely, how to align money with values. This shift from operational to intentional finance marks the difference between survival-based money management and values-based wealth building.

In this respect, friction-free systems act as behavioural scaffolding. They allow you to operate from your best self even when your energy is low or your circumstances are chaotic. This scaffolding is especially valuable during times of transition—such as starting a new job, navigating a crisis, or managing fluctuating income—when cognitive load is high and emotional regulation is taxed. Systems provide stability when motivation wavers.

Consider how this plays out for Tariq, a newly self-employed professional navigating irregular income streams. Early in his freelance career, Tariq felt overwhelmed by the need to track tax liabilities, manage inconsistent client payments, and allocate income toward multiple goals. After consulting with a financial advisor, he implemented a system in which all income flowed into a central account, from which fixed percentages were automatically distributed: taxes to a government savings account, operations to a business account, personal expenses to a current account, and surplus to investments. This envelope-style system operated invisibly in the background, reducing decision points from dozens to none. As a result, Tariq experienced less stress and had more time to focus on delivering value to his clients.

What these examples illustrate is a broader truth: systems are more compassionate than willpower. They do not ask you to be better, stronger, or more resilient—they assume that you are already doing your best, and that your best deserves support. In this way, friction-free finance becomes a form of self-care. It protects against the harsh inner critic that equates every slip with failure. It makes success the path of least resistance. And it redefines responsibility not as constant vigilance, but as smart, proactive design.

The challenge for most people is not knowing what to do—it is knowing how to make the right thing the easy thing. Friction-free systems answer this challenge by transforming best practices into default practices. They honour the complexity of modern life while simplifying the user experience. And they allow individuals to engage with their money not as a source of stress, but as a tool of clarity, alignment, and long-term purpose.

Ultimately, choosing systems over willpower is not about abdicating agency—it is about reclaiming it. It is about creating a life in which financial wellbeing is not the result of perpetual effort, but the natural outcome of intentional design. By reducing friction, we create room for focus. By automating the mundane, we free the mind for the meaningful. And by trusting systems, we build trust in ourselves—quietly, steadily, and without needing to try so hard.

Gamifying the Wealth Journey: Turning Progress into a Game

Traditional finance education is often draped in dry terminology, rigid rules, and a culture of seriousness that treats money as a subject devoid of play. The implicit message is that financial success requires sacrifice, suppression of emotion, and the embrace of boredom in the name of responsibility. But human psychology doesn't function optimally in such conditions. What we repeat, we learn. What we enjoy, we repeat. This is why gamification—designing processes to mimic the rewarding, motivating structure of games—offers an elegant and psychologically grounded alternative to the shame-based narratives often attached to money management. When applied with intention, gamification can transform the wealth-building process from a labour of obligation into a creative, emotionally engaging experience.

At its core, gamification is not about trivialising serious goals. Rather, it is about aligning with how the human brain is wired to respond to progress, reward, and feedback. Behavioural economics and neuroscience converge on one central insight: progress is addictive. When people can see tangible evidence of advancement—however small—they are more likely to persist in effort, overcome inertia, and return with greater consistency. This is why games, even when played for hours without external reward, are so effective at sustaining engagement. They provide immediate feedback, clear rules, and structured incentives. Financial systems that embed these elements become more approachable, more sustainable, and—crucially—more fun.

The psychology of fun is particularly important when it comes to money. For many, financial management is laced with anxiety, boredom, or historical trauma. Gamification provides a disarming antidote. It replaces fear with curiosity, guilt with play, and rigidity with flexibility. Take the example of visual trackers—a simple tool that provides a graphic representation of progress, such as colouring in a savings thermometer, marking days of no-spend challenges on a calendar, or filling in a "debt mountain" as it gradually erodes. These visual cues are deceptively powerful. They externalise what is typically abstract, allowing individuals to see their momentum. That visibility activates the brain's reward circuitry, particularly the release of dopamine—a neurotransmitter associated with motivation and reinforcement. What begins as a tool for measurement becomes a source of pride, and pride becomes the fuel for consistency.

This sense of progression is magnified when financial behaviours are tied to clearly defined milestones. Just as video games structure achievement through levels, quests, or badges, financial goals can be broken into meaningful steps: paying off the first £500 of debt, reaching a £1,000 emergency fund, investing the first £100, or completing a 30-day spending detox. Each milestone, once reached, offers a moment of celebration—a psychological checkpoint that reinforces capability and builds confidence. Unlike vague long-term aspirations, these gamified goals provide short-term wins that feel achievable and satisfying.

Consider Daniel, a thirty-two-year-old customer service manager who had struggled with compulsive online shopping and credit card debt. Budgeting apps and financial advice never seemed to stick until he discovered a gamified approach to spending control. He created a personal points system: each no-spend day earned ten points, each week of on-budget spending earned fifty, and every avoided impulse purchase added bonus credits. He set up a spreadsheet with colourful tabs and reward tiers—accumulating points earned him small privileges, such as a cinema night or an extra takeout. The result? He reported a 40 percent reduction in spending within three months, not because his income changed, but because his behaviour did. The system engaged his competitive instincts, gave tangible form to abstract progress, and turned discipline into play.

Digital tools are increasingly integrating gamification mechanics to capitalise on these behavioural tendencies. Apps like Qapital,

Monzo, and YNAB incorporate elements such as goal-setting visualisations, streak counters, challenges, and nudges. These features do not replace foundational financial knowledge, but they scaffold it with motivational design. A user might be nudged to save an extra £5 each time they skip a morning coffee, watch their "progress bar" grow as they inch toward a travel fund, or receive celebratory animations for reaching a goal. These might appear frivolous at first glance, but their effect is deeply grounded in the behavioural feedback loop: cue, action, reward. When the reward is immediate and tangible—even if symbolic—it strengthens the habit loop and fosters repeat engagement.

Gamification is also a powerful tool in couples' finance, where communication about money often defaults to tension, avoidance, or misalignment. Turning shared goals into collaborative games—such as a "savings sprint," where both partners aim to hit a target within a defined timeframe, or assigning light-hearted roles in budgeting tasks—can inject levity and teamwork into a space historically dominated by stress. It reframes financial planning from a battleground to a game board, where both parties are allies working toward a mutual win.

Importantly, gamifying the wealth journey is not about treating serious matters as trivial. It is about restoring a sense of agency, pleasure, and personal expression to what has too often been reduced to punitive arithmetic. This approach also resists the binary thinking that characterises much of financial discourse: either you're disciplined or irresponsible, frugal or extravagant. Games thrive in nuance. They reward creativity, experimentation, and feedback-based iteration. Financial gamification does the same. If one system fails to engage, another can be designed. The process becomes adaptive and responsive, not fixed and prescriptive.

One of the more underappreciated benefits of gamification is its capacity to dislodge perfectionism—a major barrier to consistent financial progress. Traditional financial planning often fosters an all-or-nothing mindset: if you fail to follow the budget precisely, the whole plan is considered a failure. Gamified systems, in contrast, celebrate partial success. Missing a day of savings doesn't reset the game—it simply pauses the score. This resilience encourages persistence. The goal becomes not flawless execution, but continued engagement. Over time, this builds what psychologists call self-efficacy—the belief in one's ability to influence outcomes through sustained effort.

Critically, gamifying finance also challenges deeper cultural myths about money: that it must be hard, that it's reserved for experts, or that only serious people build wealth. These narratives often exclude individuals whose learning styles, life circumstances, or emotional histories do not fit the mould of traditional financial education. Gamification opens the door to inclusivity. It meets people where they are—not where the textbook says they should be—and invites them into a new kind of relationship with money. One marked by curiosity, play, and empowerment.

This shift is particularly meaningful for younger generations raised in a digital culture of interactivity and feedback. For digital natives, static budgets on spreadsheets feel like relics. Integrating gamified financial tools into early education and adult practice offers a bridge between financial literacy and digital fluency. It speaks the language of progress bars, leaderboards, and adaptive design—making money management feel less like homework and more like a quest worth embarking on.

Ultimately, the purpose of gamifying the wealth journey is not to escape discipline, but to transform it. To replace white-knuckled restraint with purposeful engagement. To foster resilience not through shame, but through motivation. And to build financial capability not as a chore to be endured, but as a game to be played with intention, creativity, and delight.

By turning progress into play, we align with what is deepest and most enduring in human behaviour—the drive for challenge, the satisfaction of mastery, and the joy of seeing tangible progress unfold. Finance, reimagined through this lens, becomes not a test of endurance, but a field of possibility. And in that field, growth is not just achievable—it becomes inevitable.

Chapter 7
Conscious Wealth – Aligning Money with Meaning

What does it really mean to be rich? It's the sort of question that seems deceptively straightforward—almost childlike in its simplicity. But dig a little deeper, and you'll find a complexity that resists easy answers. In a culture obsessed with curated perfection, relentless output, and the numerical rituals of so-called success, our understanding of wealth has become remarkably one-dimensional. The equation usually runs something like this: more money, more luxury, more status equals more success. But does it?

Peel back that shiny veneer, and another kind of wealth begins to emerge—one measured not in digits but in depth. Time. Autonomy. A sense of peace. Integrity. Joy that isn't tied to outcomes. The ability to contribute meaningfully, without burning yourself to the ground. In this chapter, we step away from the ledger sheet and into a more expansive conversation—one that frames financial success not as mere accumulation, but as alignment. With values. With purpose. With life itself.

For far too long, we've been handed a rigid binary: you're either wealthy in the conventional, hyper-visible sense—fast cars, high ceilings, endless hustle—or you're principled, creative, mission-driven… and perpetually strapped for cash. This false choice forces individuals into painful compromises, as if soul and security cannot share the same roof. Consider the glorified "hustle millionaire"—a modern myth powered by LinkedIn posts, viral videos, and a culture that treats exhaustion as a badge of honour. Behind the montage of 4 a.m. alarms and productivity hacks is often a hollowness. A system that confuses busyness with worth, output with virtue, and leaves very little room for reflection or rest.

The consequences are real. We're told that rest is a liability. That slowing down signals weakness. That it's acceptable—noble, even—to postpone joy until we've hit some arbitrary financial milestone (and even then, joy is often elusive). Underneath it all lurks a damaging belief: that money and meaning don't mix. That choosing purpose is a luxury, not a legitimate path. That's a script worth discarding.

In truth, not only can purpose and prosperity coexist—they can fuel one another. When people align their financial decisions with their core values, something changes. The grind gives way to groundedness. The hustle morphs into clarity. Mission-driven work, far from being a charitable sideline, can be a serious engine for profit. But this requires a mental pivot—from extraction to contribution, from chasing more to creating better. It starts with asking different questions. Not just, "How can I maximise income?" but, "To what end?"

Laila's story captures this shift beautifully. Once a rising star in the investment world, she left her role to launch a mental health initiative for marginalised communities. At first, she struggled with guilt—feeling, perhaps subconsciously, that doing meaningful work should come at a financial cost. It's a belief many of us carry, often unexamined. But by treating her finances with the same care she brought to her mission—structuring fair pricing, investing in systems, scaling with intention—Laila didn't just make ends meet. She surpassed her previous income. More importantly, her work had reach, depth, and resonance. A reminder that money, when tied to meaning, has a multiplying effect.

Living in this kind of alignment means stepping beyond the budgeting models most of us were taught. The usual approach—cut costs, meet obligations, repeat—is useful in a pinch, but it rarely inspires. Conscious wealth invites a more enlivening question: How can my money reflect what truly matters to me? Suddenly, budgeting becomes something else entirely—not an exercise in restraint, but in design. You begin to allocate resources not just to obligations, but to what brings you alive: music lessons, weekend hikes, a fund for spontaneous generosity.

This, in turn, becomes a form of storytelling. Look closely at a person's budget, and you'll see a map of their values. A family that consistently sets aside money for art supplies is declaring something about who they are. A student who builds a line item for giving, even on a modest income, is rejecting the scarcity script. A retiree who funds mentorship initiatives isn't just spending—they're shaping a legacy. These aren't necessarily large gestures. But over time, they accumulate into a life that feels coherent—one where money is not separate from meaning, but an extension of it.

Which brings us to the matter of legacy. Often reduced to wills, estates, and endowments, legacy is usually treated as something to consider when life is winding down. But what if legacy isn't just about what you leave behind, but how you live today? The systems you model. The emotional tone you bring to your finances. The habits your children observe. Were your choices shaped by fear or by freedom? Did your spending reflect sufficiency or a silent panic?

Legacy also lives in the structures you build. A fair-trade business. A fund for underrepresented founders. A learning platform that levels the playing field. These are financial decisions that echo forward. Not abstract intentions, but lived expressions of what you believe. And every financial action—saving, spending, investing, giving—becomes a kind of vote. A subtle statement about the world you're helping shape.

Of course, this sort of alignment doesn't happen by accident. It asks for vigilance. For a willingness to notice—and, if necessary, rewrite—the financial narratives you've inherited. Many of us carry scripts we didn't choose: "Wanting wealth is selfish." "Money corrupts." "Better to play it safe." These are not harmless. They guide choices, often unconsciously. The work, then, is to surface them, examine them, and if they no longer serve, release them.

Tools like values-based budgeting, purpose mapping, and legacy planning are not merely theoretical. They're the groundwork of a more deliberate life. They help shift money from a source of anxiety to a medium of expression. Clarity replaces confusion. Agency takes the place of shame. And financial life becomes less a battleground and more a canvas.

This chapter is an invitation to that shift. To explore what wealth *really* means to you. To question assumptions that no longer fit. And to imagine money not as a measure of your worth, but as a way to live out your values in practice—tangibly, consciously, and with courage.

In the end, perhaps to be rich is to live in such a way that your resources—whatever their scale—sustain what you care about, extend your influence beyond your lifetime, and allow you to show up in the world with integrity. Wealth becomes less a finish line and more a reflection. Something you cultivate, not chase. Something that grows in meaning as you grow in awareness. That, surely, is the richest kind of wealth there is.

What Does "Rich" Mean to You?

What does it mean to be rich? The answer, though often assumed to be self-evident, is one of the most complex and revealing inquiries we can make about ourselves. In a culture that has long equated wealth with accumulation—of money, possessions, accolades—the concept of richness has been stripped of its nuance and depth. The prevailing definition reduces success to numerical measures: salary brackets, net worth statements, investment portfolios. But when people pause and reflect beyond societal scripts, a different truth emerges. Richness, for many, is not fundamentally about money. It is about freedom, time, inner peace, relationships, autonomy, purpose, and the ability to influence the world in ways that matter.

This dissonance between cultural messaging and personal reality is not accidental. We live in economies that are wired to measure and monetise virtually everything—from attention spans to step counts—and in doing so, they risk commodifying even the deepest aspects of life. The notion of being "rich" has therefore become a shorthand for high economic status, irrespective of emotional, mental, or existential quality. Yet as many who have attained material affluence have discovered, money alone does not guarantee meaning. The existential poverty that can accompany financial success—emptiness, isolation, burnout—is real, and increasingly acknowledged in both psychological literature and lived experience.

The challenge, then, is to reclaim the concept of wealth—to ask, with sincerity and without defaulting to external metrics: *What does rich mean to me?* This question is not rhetorical. It is diagnostic. It reveals the values that underpin financial decisions, the beliefs that inform self-worth, and the priorities that shape daily life. It invites a more expansive and personalised definition of wealth—one that can evolve across time, stages of life, and shifting circumstances.

For many, richness begins with autonomy—the freedom to make choices without financial coercion. This might look like the ability to say no to work that compromises values, to take a sabbatical without fear of ruin, or to live in a way that honours rhythm rather than routine. Autonomy allows for spaciousness—mental, emotional, and temporal. It reclaims time from the transactional and opens space for creativity, connection, and rest. In this framing, richness is not just about having more, but about needing less in order to feel secure and fulfilled.

Time, too, emerges as a primary currency of conscious wealth. Numerous studies have shown that beyond a certain income threshold—often cited around £60,000 to £75,000 annually in Western countries—additional earnings have diminishing returns on happiness. What does improve life satisfaction, however, is control over one's time. Economist Daniel Hamermesh and psychologist Ashley Whillans have both found that time affluence—the subjective sense of having enough time—correlates more strongly with wellbeing than income alone. When individuals prioritise time over money in decision-making, they report greater life satisfaction, better health, and stronger relationships. Being rich, therefore, may have more to do with unhurried breakfasts, unscheduled afternoons, and uninterrupted evenings than with high-income brackets or luxury possessions.

Peace is another undercurrent often neglected in mainstream discussions of wealth. Financial peace is not the absence of risk, but the presence of resilience. It is the inner calm that comes from living within one's means, having buffers in place, and trusting oneself to navigate uncertainty. It is also emotional—an unshaken self-worth that does not rise and fall with market fluctuations or peer comparisons. This form of richness is inward, cultivated through clarity, emotional intelligence, and a grounded sense of enoughness. For some, it means a modest but fully paid-for life. For others, it is a conscious relationship with risk that is anchored in meaning, not anxiety.

Equally significant is the concept of impact—how wealth is expressed through contribution. For many purpose-driven individuals, richness is not measured by what they can consume, but by what they can give, build, or change. Whether through philanthropy, mentorship, community work, or ethical entrepreneurship, wealth becomes a medium of influence. This is not altruism as performance, but as integration. The desire to make a difference is not separate from financial aspirations—it is part of them. In this context, being rich means having the resources and reach to leave things better than one found them.

This broader understanding of richness is evident in the lives of individuals who have consciously redefined their relationship with money. Take the example of James and Clara, a couple who left high-paying corporate roles to run a sustainable farming project. Their income halved, but their quality of life, sense of agency, and emotional wellbeing soared. For them, wealth was redefined as waking up with purpose, working in alignment with ecological values, and spending their days together with their children. Their financial choices were deliberate, not sacrificial. They chose a different kind of abundance—one rooted in coherence and contribution.

Or consider Elena, a first-generation university graduate who spent years pursuing financial stability out of survival necessity. Once she reached her target income, she realised that the relentless drive had become its own trap. She re-evaluated her goals, transitioned to part-time consulting, and allocated more time to writing and advocacy. Her new definition of rich included time to volunteer, flexibility to care for her ageing parents, and the creative freedom to work on her novel. The shift was not easy—but it was intentional. And it reoriented her entire experience of what wealth could mean.

Such stories are not anomalies. They reflect a growing consciousness that financial success, divorced from meaning, is not success at all. The movement toward conscious wealth is grounded in this awareness. It does not reject money, nor does it romanticise struggle.

Rather, it invites discernment. It encourages individuals to define, for themselves, what they are actually pursuing—and whether the pursuit is delivering what it promised.

This redefinition also has practical implications. It informs how people structure their budgets, plan their careers, and measure progress. If richness is defined as time freedom, then decisions about debt, housing, and work hours will reflect that priority. If peace is the goal, then minimising financial chaos takes precedence over maximising earnings. If contribution is central, then spending and investing will lean toward values-aligned choices. This alignment breeds integrity—not the moral kind, but the structural kind: wholeness, consistency, and inner congruence.

Ultimately, asking *What does rich mean to me?* is not about arriving at a fixed answer. It is about cultivating a practice of inquiry—one that evolves as life unfolds. It is about resisting inherited definitions and crafting personal ones. It is about ensuring that financial goals are not just impressive, but resonant. That the pursuit of wealth does not come at the cost of the very things it was meant to secure.

In reframing richness as multidimensional—spanning time, peace, autonomy, impact, and joy—we reclaim financial life from the tyranny of metrics and root it in meaning. This is not a rejection of ambition or prosperity. It is a deepening of it. It is the realisation that the most valuable forms of wealth are often the least visible—and that the richest lives are not always the loudest.

To live richly, then, is to live deliberately. To name what matters. To structure money not around what society tells you to value, but around what you *actually* value. And to let that clarity inform every choice—from the mundane to the monumental. In doing so, wealth becomes not a destination, but a reflection. Not a possession, but a practice. Not merely what you have, but how fully, freely, and meaningfully you live.

The Myth of the Hustle Millionaire: Challenging Toxic Productivity and the Cult of Relentless Work

The cultural figure of the hustle millionaire—relentless, always grinding, never satisfied—has become a modern archetype. He or she rises at 4 a.m., dominates the day with an impossible workload, and rests only long enough to post another motivational quote about sacrifice. This figure is glorified on social media, held up as a blueprint in entrepreneurial circles, and paraded in bestselling books that equate suffering with success. But beneath the veneer of productivity lies a troubling reality: the hustle millionaire is, more often than not, a mirage. This archetype is not only unrealistic but deeply damaging, perpetuating myths about wealth creation, self-worth, and the path to a meaningful life.

At first glance, the ethos of hustling appears empowering. It champions effort, resilience, and personal agency. But when taken to extremes—as it often is—it becomes a form of performance anxiety masked as ambition. It teaches people to conflate self-exhaustion with dedication, to glorify burnout as a badge of honour, and to equate rest with laziness. In this worldview, time is not a dimension to be lived in but a commodity to be optimised. Life is reduced to outputs. Relationships, health, and inner life become secondary—sacrifices at the altar of financial ascent.

This cultural obsession with hustle reflects a wider pathology of overwork that has taken root across industries and demographics. In her groundbreaking book *Do Nothing*, Celeste Headlee outlines how modern Western societies have normalised busyness to such an extent that our self-worth is measured by productivity. Hustle culture feeds this pathology by perpetuating the belief that only through total devotion—measured in hours, not effectiveness—can one achieve meaningful wealth. This ideology borrows heavily from the Protestant work ethic, reframed through the lens of modern capitalism and turbocharged by digital platforms that never sleep.

Yet when we scrutinise the data, the myth starts to crack. According to a 2021 study by Harvard Business School, overwork does not equate to increased output beyond a certain threshold. After around 50 hours per week, productivity declines sharply. More importantly, the study found no significant correlation between long work hours and long-term financial success for most individuals. In fact, those who prioritised strategic work, emotional regulation, and relational capital often outperformed those who merely worked more hours. The hustle millionaire, it seems, may be outworked by the well-rested strategist.

Real-world stories further illuminate this. Consider the tech start-up founder who raised millions in venture capital but suffered a breakdown after two years of round-the-clock work. Or the social media influencer preaching hustle while outsourcing much of their content creation and support staff. These are not anomalies—they are features of a culture that prioritises optics over wellbeing, velocity over sustainability. The visible success stories often conceal invisible scaffolding: generational wealth, supportive partners, professional networks, mental health support—all of which contradict the lone-wolf, grind-it-out narrative.

This myth also reinforces deeply unequal assumptions about access and opportunity. It suggests that anyone can become wealthy with enough grit, thereby obscuring the structural advantages that undergird many success stories. Socioeconomic background, racial privilege, gender dynamics, and access to education are often conveniently omitted from hustle narratives. The message becomes not only misleading but cruel: if you're not succeeding, it must be because you're not grinding hard enough.

Psychologically, the toll is steep. Hustle culture erodes boundaries between work and life, leading to chronic stress, anxiety, and identity diffusion. When people define themselves primarily through productivity, any pause in output feels like an existential threat. Burnout becomes not a glitch in the system, but an expected rite of passage. According to the World Health Organization, burnout is now recognised as an occupational phenomenon, and its prevalence has surged among those immersed in performance-driven environments. The hustle myth exacerbates this by pathologising balance and sanctifying exhaustion.

There is, however, a growing countercurrent—one that seeks to replace hustle with alignment, and relentless striving with conscious design. This shift does not reject ambition but reframes it. It invites individuals to question the purpose of their work, the values behind their goals, and the cost of their definitions of success. In this paradigm, wealth is not measured solely in financial metrics but in freedom, integrity, creativity, and contribution.

A case in point is Priya, a successful marketing consultant who scaled her business while working 30 hours per week. Her approach was not about grinding but about intentionality: choosing high-leverage projects, nurturing client relationships, delegating effectively, and preserving her mental and physical health as strategic priorities. Her wealth-building process was slower than her peers', but it was sustainable, aligned, and fulfilling. More importantly, she still had energy for her family, her art, and her community. She is part of a new vanguard redefining what it means to be wealthy—not by intensity, but by integrity.

The rejection of hustle culture is also visible in workplace trends. The rise of remote work, flexible schedules, and the "quiet quitting" phenomenon all reflect a growing desire to reclaim time and autonomy. People are beginning to ask: If work is consuming the best of my energy, my presence, my health—what, exactly, am I earning? And is the trade-off worth it?

From a financial perspective, the answer is increasingly no. True wealth creation is more often the result of clarity, systems, and leverage than brute effort. This is the essence of strategic finance: using time wisely, investing deliberately, building assets that generate income independent of labour. These require focus, yes—but not martyrdom. The most effective wealth builders are often not the most exhausted, but the most clear-headed. They understand that the point of wealth is not just to have more, but to live more.

To dismantle the hustle myth, we must first interrogate our own internalised beliefs. Where did we learn that success must hurt? Who benefits from our overwork? What stories have we absorbed about effort, value, and identity? Only by confronting these questions can we begin to design financial lives that are truly our own.

It also requires a cultural re-education. We must stop idolising figures who glorify self-neglect in the name of ambition. We must broaden the narrative of success to include those who build quietly, slowly, and mindfully. We must teach younger generations that rest is not laziness, that balance is not mediocrity, and that purpose is not incompatible with profit.

This is not a call for complacency. Ambition has its place. But ambition without alignment becomes addiction—an endless loop of striving with no arrival. Conscious wealth challenges that loop. It asks: What am I building? Why does it matter? Who do I become in the process? And is there a way to design a life where work supports, rather than supplants, wellbeing?

The myth of the hustle millionaire has had its time. Its script is fraying. In its place, we are invited to write new narratives—ones that honour energy, meaning, sustainability, and joy. The new millionaires are not those who grind endlessly, but those who live deliberately. Not those who sacrifice everything for status, but those who align money with freedom, purpose, and peace. The grind is optional. Conscious wealth is not.

Money and Purpose: Can They Coexist?

For generations, a deep cultural divide has persisted between purpose and profit—as though meaning must come at the expense of money, and financial success must be severed from soul-aligned work. The myth of the "starving artist" and the trope of the "broke healer" are not simply cautionary tales; they are identities that have been absorbed into the collective psyche, reinforcing the idea that to be spiritually, creatively, or ethically fulfilled is to be financially compromised. Yet this false dichotomy has never served humanity well. It disempowers those doing some of the most vital work in the world and narrows the definition of wealth to those who pursue it without regard for mission. It is time to retire this outdated narrative and ask, with clarity and courage: can money and purpose not only coexist, but support and amplify one another?

The short answer is yes—but only when we unlearn the conditioning that treats them as opposites.

The notion that meaningful work must be financially marginalised stems from centuries of religious, philosophical, and economic narratives that idealised sacrifice and vilified profit. In many spiritual traditions, renunciation was considered a moral virtue, while money was associated with greed or corruption. This seeped into the language of creative and helping professions, where suffering for one's craft or clients became a symbol of authenticity. These narratives may have once been anchored in specific historical contexts, but they have since calcified into limiting beliefs that no longer serve the modern world.

Today, mission-driven professionals—therapists, artists, coaches, educators, wellness practitioners, non-profit leaders—continue to underprice, overdeliver, and self-sacrifice, believing that financial abundance somehow taints the purity of their purpose. They avoid charging adequately, invest poorly in their own growth, and delay personal financial planning, all while pouring energy into transformational work. This creates a cycle of burnout, scarcity, and, ultimately, reduced impact. When purpose-led individuals are financially disempowered, their capacity to serve sustainably diminishes. Purpose suffers. The work itself suffers. And the wider community is left poorer for it.

This is not simply a theoretical critique. It is borne out in countless real-world examples. Consider Maya, a trauma-informed yoga teacher and mental health advocate. For years, she kept her rates well below industry standard, driven by a belief that healing should be "accessible to all." While noble in intention, her pricing model left her chronically exhausted, unable to scale, and ultimately forced her to take on side jobs that drained her creative energy. When she eventually restructured her offerings—introducing scalable group programmes, raising her one-on-one rates, and offering scholarships to maintain accessibility—her income tripled in twelve months. More importantly, she reported feeling more energised, focused, and resourced to support others. Her purpose did not suffer from profitability—it was enabled by it.

There are increasing numbers of examples like Maya. Social enterprises, ethical brands, and heart-centred service providers are beginning to break the binary between money and mission. They are proving that purpose and profit are not competing forces, but potential partners. The key lies in reimagining the business model—not as a cold, capitalist structure, but as a values-aligned vehicle for expansion. Profit, in this context, is not about personal greed but about sustainability, sovereignty, and scaled impact.

Part of this reframing involves reclaiming the moral neutrality of money. Money, in itself, is not inherently virtuous or corrupt. It is a tool—an amplifier of intention. When held by exploitative forces, it can indeed do great harm. But in the hands of those committed to healing, justice, and transformation, money becomes a force multiplier. It allows ideas to become institutions, conversations to become campaigns, and one-on-one support to become community-scale solutions.

The misconception that purpose and money are incompatible also stems from a misunderstanding of value. Many purpose-driven professionals equate pricing with exploitation. But price is not merely a number—it is a signal. It communicates the value of the work, the boundary of the practitioner, and the commitment of the recipient. When pricing is aligned with the true energetic, emotional, and transformational value being delivered, it becomes an expression of integrity. Undercharging, by contrast, can unconsciously communicate undervaluation—not only of the service but of the self.

This is especially critical in helping professions, where practitioners often experience "compassion fatigue"—an emotional depletion resulting from sustained giving without adequate replenishment. Charging fairly is not just about income; it is about energy hygiene. It is about honouring the reciprocal nature of all healing and growth work. When service providers are financially secure, they are better equipped to hold space, create boundaries, and deliver lasting impact.

Moreover, profitability enables scale. A purpose-driven business or mission can only reach so far when it is limited by the personal labour of its founder. Financial resources allow for delegation, automation, strategic partnerships, and the creation of products or services that extend beyond the founder's direct input. This moves the mission from fragile to resilient, from one-off to institutional, from reactive to visionary.

Consider the case of "SoulWell," a coaching collective founded by two former social workers. Initially, they offered low-cost individual sessions and barely broke even. Within two years, they had transitioned to a model that included high-ticket group intensives, corporate emotional intelligence programmes, and licensed curriculum for other professionals. This allowed them not only to increase their income but to employ ten other purpose-driven coaches and serve thousands of clients. Their profitability did not dilute their mission—it magnified it.

Importantly, this shift also involves redefining the image of the purpose-led individual. The "starving artist" and the "broke healer" must be consciously replaced with new archetypes: the abundant creator, the empowered change agent, the well-resourced visionary. These are individuals who do not apologise for their ambition, who see money as a tool rather than a threat, and who understand that the most effective way to dismantle unjust systems is not to opt out of wealth but to redirect it.

This reframing must also extend to education and mentorship. Emerging professionals in values-driven fields should be taught not just the skills of their craft but the financial competencies that allow their work to thrive. Business literacy, pricing psychology, ethical marketing, and wealth mindset are not luxuries—they are necessities. Without them, too many talented individuals leave their fields out of exhaustion or financial desperation, depriving the world of needed service.

Ultimately, money and purpose coexist most powerfully when both are grounded in clarity. Clarity about values, about boundaries, about the kind of life one is building and the impact one is creating. In this context, financial growth is not an indulgence—it is an act of alignment. It allows the purposeful life to be not a precarious balancing act, but a sustainable ecosystem—where resources flow, energy is protected, and the work expands beyond the individual.

This shift is not merely ideological. It is structural. It requires changes in how we educate, how we price, how we build systems, and how we tell stories. But it begins at the personal level. By choosing to unhook from inherited scripts of scarcity and martyrdom, purpose-driven individuals can reclaim their financial power—not as a betrayal of their mission, but as its foundation.

When we allow money and purpose to coexist, we create a new paradigm—one where doing good is not only sustainable but prosperous, and where financial freedom is not a detour from purpose, but its most powerful ally. The world does not need more exhausted idealists. It needs energised, well-resourced, strategically empowered visionaries who understand that purpose without profit is a whisper—but with it, becomes a roar.

Creating a Purpose-Aligned Budget: How to Budget Not Just for Survival—But for Joy, Growth, and Giving

For many, the word *budget* conjures images of constraint, scarcity, and denial—a tightly controlled spreadsheet meant to limit desire and impose discipline. In popular discourse, budgeting is framed as a reactive measure, primarily concerned with cutting costs and curbing consumption. But what if a budget could do more than protect us from financial shortfall? What if, instead of just preserving our capacity to survive, it became a proactive framework for living more deliberately—for directing resources toward joy, personal growth, and meaningful contribution? A purpose-aligned budget begins with this premise: that our money is not just a means of protection, but an instrument of expression.

This reorientation challenges many of the traditional assumptions embedded in mainstream financial advice. Most budgeting methods operate from a deficit mindset—categorising every expenditure as a drain on resources, and treating non-essential spending as indulgent or irresponsible. By contrast, a purpose-aligned budget reframes spending as a reflection of values. Rather than asking *What can I afford?* it poses the deeper question: *What matters most to me, and how can my finances support that?*

At the heart of this approach lies the concept of intentional allocation. Every pound spent or saved carries energy—it signals what we prioritise, what we are building, and what we believe we deserve. A conventional budget often separates necessity from desire, with survival needs at the centre and joy relegated to the margins. But this binary division is not only emotionally unsatisfying—it is psychologically unsustainable. Human beings are not purely economic units; we are complex, emotional creatures who thrive when our values and resources are in alignment. A budget that neglects this emotional and psychological dimension ultimately fails to inspire long-term engagement.

Consider the case of Darren, a secondary school teacher who had followed a strict zero-based budget for over a decade. His finances were technically in order—bills were paid, debt was minimal, and his savings were growing. Yet Darren felt persistently resentful of his financial routine. Joyful experiences—travel, hobbies, meals out—were treated as frivolous costs, and his sense of purpose, once tied to education, had become stifled by a rigid money script. After attending a financial wellness workshop, he restructured his budget to include three new categories: "Adventure," "Learning," and "Impact." These were small allocations, but they transformed his relationship with money. Travel funds enabled him to volunteer abroad during summer holidays; learning funds supported a part-time degree in educational leadership; and his impact category allowed him to regularly donate to causes aligned with his values. His financial life became animated by meaning, not just mechanics.

This shift illustrates a crucial principle: budgets must be personal, not just practical. Traditional budgets often follow fixed percentage guidelines—allocate 50% for needs, 30% for wants, 20% for savings. While helpful as a starting point, these templates rarely reflect the full complexity of an individual's life, values, and aspirations. A purpose-aligned budget does not begin with formulas; it begins with reflection. What brings you joy? What experiences have shaped your growth? What kind of impact do you wish to have on your community, your family, the world? These are not financial questions—they are existential ones. Yet how you answer them will determine the shape of your financial reality.

Practical implementation of a purpose-aligned budget involves moving beyond static categories like "rent" or "groceries" and creating dynamic categories that reflect value-driven intentions. This may mean introducing labels such as "Creativity," "Healing," "Connection," or "Legacy." For a young parent, allocating funds for monthly date nights may be as crucial to their wellbeing as food or transport. For an entrepreneur, setting aside capital for experimentation—even if it doesn't yield immediate ROI—may represent a commitment to innovation and growth. The categories themselves matter less than the consciousness behind them.

There is growing evidence to support this values-based approach. In behavioural economics, research consistently shows that people are more likely to follow through on financial plans that feel personally meaningful. A 2020 study published in the *Journal of Consumer Psychology* found that individuals who linked financial behaviours to intrinsic goals—such as personal development or contribution—demonstrated higher engagement and greater financial resilience over time. The study's authors concluded that emotional salience, not simply logical structure, was the key differentiator in budgeting success.

Crucially, a purpose-aligned budget also carves out intentional space for giving. In conventional models, charitable donations are often treated as optional—something to consider *if there's anything left over.* But in a purpose-led financial philosophy, giving is not peripheral; it is foundational. Giving reinforces the belief in sufficiency. It expands one's sense of agency and abundance. And it serves as a tangible expression of alignment—bridging internal values with external impact.

Take the example of Anjali, a freelance graphic designer who once saw charitable giving as financially out of reach. After attending a purpose and money retreat, she began allocating 5% of her income to a "Compassion Fund." Sometimes it went to formal charities, other times to personal causes—covering a friend's vet bill, buying groceries for a single mother, or supporting refugee art collectives. Over time, this small act of generosity reshaped her sense of self. She no longer felt like someone just getting by—she felt like a contributor. Her confidence grew, her work flourished, and interestingly, her income doubled within two years. While correlation is not causation, her case reflects a common pattern: when people align their finances with their values, they often attract greater clarity, confidence, and opportunity.

This is not to suggest that budgeting should ignore financial discipline. A purpose-aligned budget still honours the foundational principles of sound money management—spending less than one earns, avoiding high-interest debt, saving for the future. But it does so in a way that is emotionally resonant. It replaces guilt with intention, deprivation with discernment, and rigidity with fluidity. It also acknowledges that seasons of life require different emphases. A recent graduate may need to focus more on stability; a mid-career professional might emphasise growth and giving; a retiree may prioritise peace and legacy. A flexible, purpose-led structure allows these shifts without shame.

Technology can support this transformation. Many digital budgeting tools now allow for customisable categories, notes, and reminders—making it easier to design budgets that reflect personal narratives. Apps like YNAB (You Need A Budget), Goodbudget, and Monarch empower users to move beyond mere tracking and toward intentional design. When paired with periodic reflection—monthly check-ins, annual reviews—these tools become not just ledgers, but mirrors. They show not only where the money went, but whether it went where it mattered.

Ultimately, a budget is a form of storytelling. It tells the story of what we care about, what we believe is possible, and how we move through the world. A purpose-aligned budget ensures that this story is not written by default or dictated by external pressures, but authored consciously, in a voice that is wholly our own. It transforms money from a source of stress into a medium of self-expression. And it redefines wealth not as an accumulation of currency, but as the consistent alignment of our resources with our deepest truths.

To budget for joy, growth, and giving is not naive—it is visionary. It acknowledges that financial health is not merely a question of spreadsheets, but of soul. It asks that we consider not only how much we have, but how fully we are living. And it challenges us to use money not just as a tool for protection, but as a canvas for purpose. In doing so, it invites us to experience finance not as a constraint, but as a liberating design—one where every line item is an act of alignment, and every transaction a quiet expression of what we truly value.

Building Your Financial Legacy: Thinking Beyond You

Legacy is a concept often relegated to the twilight years—spoken of in hushed tones by financial planners and estate lawyers, neatly summarised in wills and legal documents. But legacy is far more than the orderly distribution of assets after death. It is the long shadow our values, decisions, and actions cast across time. In financial terms, a legacy is not simply what we leave behind, but how we shape the future through the way we engage with money today. Building a financial legacy, therefore, is not a passive event that happens at life's end—it is an active process of intentional design that reflects how we live, what we prioritise, and how we choose to contribute beyond ourselves.

At its most fundamental, a financial legacy asks a provocative question: what do you want your money to do when you're no longer here to guide it? This inquiry cuts to the core of wealth's deeper purpose. It challenges the prevailing notion that financial planning ends with personal security or retirement goals. Instead, it pushes us to consider a broader, intergenerational perspective—one that integrates stewardship, vision, and impact.

For many, financial legacy begins with family. Ensuring that loved ones are supported—whether through inheritance, educational funds, or housing stability—is a natural and noble aspiration. But even within this context, legacy can be either reactive or intentional. A reactive legacy is driven by default behaviours: accumulating wealth with the hope that it "trickles down" meaningfully. An intentional legacy, by contrast, is designed with clarity and communication. It involves articulating not just *what* will be passed on, but *why*. It invites conversations with children or beneficiaries about values, financial literacy, and the responsibility that accompanies resources.

Consider the example of Malcolm, a second-generation entrepreneur who built a successful property portfolio. Rather than simply leaving assets to his three children, he created a family foundation with clear philanthropic objectives and involved each child in its operation. From an early age, his children participated in decisions about which causes to support, how to assess impact, and how to balance charitable giving with financial sustainability. This structure served not only as a mechanism for wealth transfer, but as a platform for ethical development, civic engagement, and strategic thinking. For Malcolm, legacy was not about creating passive recipients—it was about cultivating stewards of value.

This shift—from transfer to transformation—is at the heart of purpose-driven legacy planning. It moves beyond the mechanics of inheritance and into the realm of influence. It acknowledges that money, when passed without context, can be destabilising. Sudden windfalls—particularly among heirs unprepared to manage them—often result in diminished wealth, fractured relationships, or unintended dependency. A 2018 study by the Williams Group found that 70% of wealthy families lose their wealth by the second generation, and 90% by the third. The root cause is rarely technical. It is relational: lack of communication, misalignment of values, and the absence of a shared vision.

To build a lasting financial legacy, therefore, one must first establish a living philosophy of money. This involves interrogating core beliefs: What is money *for*? What role should it play in the lives of those who inherit it? What values should guide its use? Articulating these principles in writing—or better yet, through lived practice—provides an essential compass for future generations. Legacy, in this sense, becomes less about transmission and more about continuity.

For some, financial legacy extends beyond the family unit and into the community. Endowments, foundations, and bequests are common vehicles, but smaller, more personal acts of generosity can also leave enduring imprints. Consider Amina, a retired educator who established a micro-scholarship programme for first-generation university students in her local area. Though the individual awards were modest—£1,000 per student—the cumulative effect was profound. Dozens of students graduated who might otherwise have dropped out. Several returned as mentors and donors themselves. Amina's legacy was not measured by monetary scale, but by ripple effect—what behavioural scientists refer to as "social return on investment."

Equally significant is the idea of entrepreneurial legacy. Founders and creators have a unique opportunity to embed values into the DNA of their businesses. Structures such as employee ownership models, social enterprises, or B Corporations formalise this intent. But even absent legal frameworks, business owners can design succession plans, equity models, or revenue-sharing systems that reflect their broader aspirations. For example, Luis, a restaurateur passionate about food justice, transitioned his business to a worker co-op before retiring. In doing so, he not only preserved the livelihood of his staff, but codified a principle of empowerment into the enterprise itself.

Legacy, then, is not bound by legal instruments alone. It lives in systems, stories, and relationships. It asks not only *What will I leave behind?* but also *What will continue to grow because I once acted?* And crucially: *Will those who follow me know what to do with what I've built?*

This is where financial education plays a pivotal role. Passing on assets without accompanying knowledge is akin to handing someone a ship without navigation tools. A legacy built on wisdom—on teaching children and community members about investing, giving, budgeting, and ethical decision-making—creates lasting agency. In fact, the most effective legacy plans often combine three elements: financial capital, human capital, and social capital. Financial capital is the money itself. Human capital includes education, character, and skills. Social capital encompasses networks, reputation, and goodwill. Together, they form a multidimensional legacy—one that resists erosion and compounds in impact.

One often overlooked aspect of financial legacy is the emotional resonance it can carry. Money is rarely neutral. It is laden with stories—of struggle, triumph, sacrifice, fear, and pride. When people leave behind unspoken narratives, they create room for misinterpretation or conflict. But when individuals consciously narrate their financial journey—the decisions they made, the mistakes they learned from, the intentions they held—they offer something far more valuable than assets. They offer perspective. A letter of financial intent, shared alongside a will, can serve as a bridge between generations, grounding future decisions in a lineage of thoughtfulness.

Importantly, building a financial legacy need not require great wealth. It requires great intentionality. Whether one leaves behind £1,000 or £1 million, the impact is shaped by the clarity of purpose. A single act—a donation, a lesson, a conversation—can catalyse change far beyond its immediate context. As systems thinkers often note, small shifts in one part of a system can produce large shifts in the whole.

Creating a purpose-aligned financial legacy begins with a set of courageous questions: What do I stand for? What do I want to endure? What mechanisms—financial, relational, structural—can I put in place to ensure that my influence continues with integrity? These questions are not merely logistical; they are spiritual. They ask us to reckon with our impermanence and to plant seeds whose fruit we may never eat.

Yet in this planting, there is hope. Hope that our resources, however modest, can be steered toward life-affirming ends. Hope that those who follow us will be equipped not just with money, but with meaning. And hope that the story of our financial life will not end at our death, but continue—as a source of guidance, inspiration, and possibility for generations to come.

A financial legacy, ultimately, is not about being remembered—it is about being useful. It is about designing money to outlive ego, to serve others, and to extend the arc of one's values beyond a single lifetime. That is the power of legacy. Not in what it preserves, but in what it makes possible.

Chapter 8
Financial Expansion—Playing a Bigger Game

At some juncture in our financial journeys, a question quietly but insistently emerges: what if we stopped managing money merely to get by—and began managing it to grow, to expand? It's a pivotal shift, one that often slips under the radar. Many of us, shaped by lean times, learn discipline, prudence, and a kind of cautious ingenuity. Those traits serve us well when scarcity rules the day. Yet, cling to them too tightly once opportunity arises, and they can become shackles rather than tools. Moving from a survival mindset into one of vision demands more than new strategies—it requires a psychological turning point. Suddenly, the game isn't just about avoiding loss but about cultivating abundance. It calls for a readiness to stop shrinking in fear and instead step boldly into clarity, courage, and purposeful intention.

This chapter wrestles with that very transformation. It marks the moment when we stop fretting over "How do I avoid running out of money?" and start daring to ask, "What does it mean to truly thrive—and to contribute meaningfully along the way?" For too many, particularly those carrying the heavy echoes of financial trauma, systemic barriers, or ancestral scarcity narratives, the survival mindset lingers long after circumstances improve. Bank accounts may grow, yet internal compasses remain stuck in crisis mode. People undercharge, shy away from opportunities, or quietly dim their ambitions to fit outdated self-beliefs. None of this is irrational—it's the nervous system's automatic way of seeking safety. But it's also a roadblock to flourishing.

To play a larger financial game, one must begin by rewriting these mental scripts that keep us small. Not by tossing caution aside, but by recognising that lasting wealth creation calls for a vision-driven approach—not merely reactive management. Survival mode is about safety. Vision mode seeks coherence—a financial life that aligns with one's values, gifts, and long-term dreams. This is no reckless gamble; it is bravery. Bravery with money.

And yet, bravery often wrestles with guilt. Especially for those committed to ethical living, the yearning for financial abundance can stir unease. "Is it right to want more? Am I selfish? How will others see me if I succeed?" These are genuine concerns, especially in a world riddled with inequality. But guilt is rarely a helpful compass. Left unexamined, it traps people in a double bind, caught between wanting to prosper and fearing disconnection from their principles or community. The outcome? Self-sabotage—a pattern of avoidance, delay, or an invisible ceiling placed on ambition.

Welcoming wealth without guilt demands a shift in ethics. Wealth, in itself, is not immoral; its character depends on how it is earned, stewarded, and shared. When money flows from aligned actions, is handled with integrity, and is directed toward life-enhancing purposes, it transforms into a kind of power—a power that nurtures both the individual and the collective. Wealth is ethical when it is intentional. And purpose, in turn, becomes scalable when backed by resources.

This leads us to what might be called the circle of expansion. It starts with mindset: a turn toward possibility, sufficiency, and deliberate growth. This mental shift sparks different behaviours—taking measured risks, asserting oneself, pursuing higher-impact opportunities. These steps often translate into increased resources, which unlock further possibilities: better systems, stronger networks, new investments, partnerships. Those options then reinforce the mindset, bolstering the belief that expansion is not only attainable but sustainable. This virtuous loop stands in stark contrast to the scarcity spiral, where fear contracts, breeding yet more fear. The circle of expansion thrives on courage, clarity, and forward momentum.

Of course, courage isn't the absence of fear; it's the resolve to act despite it. Nowhere is this clearer than in financial risk-taking. Launching a venture, exploring new investment classes, negotiating pay—these acts almost always involve stepping into uncertainty. Yet, culturally, our lessons about risk skew heavily toward fear of loss rather than pursuit of gain. Cognitive biases like loss aversion and confirmation bias further distort how we assess risk, nudging us toward excessive caution.

Financial expansion requires mastering the art of calculated risk—risks that align with our aims, are informed by research, and rest on a foundation of self-trust. That means building buffers to weather setbacks and cultivating emotional resilience to tolerate the inevitable discomfort. It means moving beyond a binary "safe or unsafe" mindset toward a more nuanced spectrum, where small experiments yield data, and data nurtures confidence.

Take Priyanka's example. Once a mid-level executive, she stepped away from corporate life to launch a consultancy devoted to inclusive leadership. Early on, pricing her services was a battleground—fear of rejection, or appearing greedy, held her back. But through investing in coaching, nurturing strategic relationships, and piloting her programmes, she gained clarity on her worth. Her fees rose accordingly, as did her impact. Today, her firm not only serves global clients but also sponsors scholarships for women of colour leaders. Her growth didn't require reckless abandon—just a reframing of risk as creative courage.

The environment we craft around our finances matters immensely. Much like athletes shape their training spaces to foster excellence, so too must those pursuing financial expansion cultivate surroundings that support their vision. This extends beyond physical spaces to digital tools, habits, and relationships. Who we choose to spend time with, the content we consume, and even the language we use around money all colour our financial realities.

For example, automatic savings apps, intuitive investment platforms, and visual progress trackers reduce decision fatigue and make forward movement tangible. Connecting with peers who embody integrity and abundance helps normalise a mindset of possibility, shaking loose old limiting scripts. Even shifting from "I can't afford that" to "How can I make that happen?" can change the atmosphere from scarcity to opportunity.

Designing a supportive financial environment also means attending to our internal architecture. Our nervous systems are conditioned by inherited and learned patterns about what feels safe or acceptable. Financial growth often nudges us beyond comfort zones. Learning to discern when discomfort signals growth rather than danger is crucial. Tools such as somatic awareness, mindset coaching, journaling, or visualisation can help recalibrate internal settings, enabling external expansion.

Ultimately, playing a bigger financial game isn't about chasing more for its own sake. It's about widening our thinking, sharpening our strategy, and deepening our courage. It means recognising that money isn't a separate beast but woven tightly into our creative, relational, and spiritual lives. Wealth is not a destination—it's a tool, one that can amplify either our fears or our purpose, depending on how we wield it.

This chapter invites you to move beyond minimalist survival and into intentional growth. Not to hoard wealth, but to harness it. Not to pursue status, but to claim agency. It's a call to dismantle inherited ceilings, rewrite outdated scripts, and build financial ecosystems that nurture expansion with grace.

Financial expansion isn't reserved for a select few. It's open to anyone ready to think differently, act with intention, and stay grounded in purpose. It asks us to see money not just as survival, but as a medium of self-expression and impact. To play bigger isn't to gamble—it's to design. With precision. With courage. And with the quiet confidence that you are no longer merely managing money, but mobilising it—toward a future shaped by your highest intentions.

From Survival Mode to Vision Mode: Reclaiming Financial Agency Through Strategic Living

Most people don't make their earliest financial decisions from a place of calm reflection—they make them from necessity. Bills need paying, groceries need buying, debt needs servicing. In these moments, money management becomes a form of firefighting. The aim is not to build; it is to survive. This is what is known as *survival mode*—a psychological and behavioural state in which financial thinking is reactive, short-term, and fear-driven. While often essential in periods of genuine hardship, survival mode can become a self-perpetuating state, long outliving the original crisis. Many continue to operate from it even when the immediate danger has passed, never realising that their internal financial compass is still set to "emergency." The alternative—*vision mode*—requires an entirely different mindset. It replaces panic with perspective, scarcity with strategy, and urgency with intentionality.

Survival mode is not inherently irrational. It often reflects very real conditions: unstable income, systemic inequality, unexpected health issues, or intergenerational poverty. It is a mode born of necessity and honed through repetition. In fact, neuroscientific research confirms that when individuals face persistent financial instability, the brain's cognitive bandwidth is impaired. Chronic stress narrows focus to the present, reducing capacity for long-term planning or risk assessment. A 2013 study published in *Science* found that financial scarcity can reduce cognitive function to the equivalent of losing 13 IQ points—a deficit akin to the effects of sleep deprivation.

In other words, survival mode is not a character flaw. It is a neurological and emotional adaptation to precarity. But what begins as adaptive can become restrictive. People accustomed to crisis often find it difficult to transition to stability—even when their circumstances change. Habits like hoarding cash, avoiding investment, under-earning, or financial procrastination may persist because they feel familiar. The nervous system, having internalised fear as a baseline, interprets calm as risk. Even the idea of "vision" can feel indulgent or dangerous to someone whose financial identity has been forged through constraint.

This is why the shift to vision mode is not simply about income. It is about *permission*—the internal permission to think bigger, to plan further, and to act proactively rather than defensively. Vision mode invites individuals to ask: *What am I building? What kind of life do I want my money to support? What would it look like to design my finances rather than endure them?*

To make this transition, one must first recognise the signs of being stuck in survival thinking. These may include constant financial anxiety even when bills are paid, an inability to make long-term plans, feeling guilty about spending on joy or creativity, or a hyper-focus on "playing it safe" that borders on paralysis. From this awareness, new habits can be cultivated—not through shame, but through structured support.

A useful case study is Sofia, a graphic designer who had spent most of her twenties under-employed and living paycheque to paycheque. By her early thirties, her freelance business had grown steadily, and she had six months of expenses saved. Yet she still avoided looking at her bank account, refused to raise her rates, and told herself she was "bad with money." In therapy, she realised that her financial behaviours were anchored not in logic, but in fear—specifically, a fear of returning to scarcity. With guidance, she began implementing vision-based strategies: setting quarterly income goals, automating her savings, investing in skill development, and planning a sabbatical to travel. Her financial reality hadn't changed overnight—but her posture toward money had. She had moved from defence to design.

Vision mode does not negate caution. It simply repositions it. Rather than avoiding risk altogether, vision-oriented thinkers learn to take *informed* risks in service of longer-term outcomes. They understand the concept of opportunity cost—not just in terms of money, but time, energy, and potential. They know that constantly playing not to lose is different from playing to win. In practical terms, this may mean choosing to invest in a business, career change, or asset class even if the decision feels mildly uncomfortable—because discomfort is no longer confused with danger.

Part of embracing vision mode is building structures that replace willpower with systems. Survival mode often relies on mental micromanagement: juggling bills, remembering due dates, reacting to financial events as they arise. This creates cognitive fatigue and reinforces stress. Vision mode, by contrast, externalises decision-making. Budgets are pre-set to reflect values. Payments and savings are automated. Financial reviews happen on schedule. These systems don't eliminate uncertainty—but they reduce the emotional burden of navigating it.

Visionary financial strategies also incorporate time differently. Survival mode focuses exclusively on the present or the short-term future. Vision mode integrates multiple timelines—planning for five, ten, even twenty years ahead. This isn't about rigid forecasting; it's about directionality. It creates a financial narrative that aligns with life's deeper goals—owning a home, creating generational wealth, supporting a cause, retiring early, funding education, or taking creative risks. Without such a narrative, money becomes aimless. With it, it becomes directional.

A particularly transformative feature of vision mode is its emphasis on *agency*. In survival mode, the locus of control is external: markets crash, rent increases, clients disappear. People feel at the mercy of circumstance. In vision mode, control is internalised—not in the sense of denying reality, but in the sense of reclaiming influence. The question shifts from "What's happening to me?" to "How can I respond strategically to what's happening?" This cognitive shift restores autonomy and expands perceived options.

Yet the leap from survival to vision often requires bridging a chasm of emotional resistance. Many people carry internalised beliefs that limit their capacity to think expansively about money. They fear being judged, losing community, or becoming someone they don't recognise. There may also be inherited scripts about money being dangerous, corrupting, or morally suspect. Addressing these scripts—through coaching, community, or introspection—is essential. Vision mode is not merely financial; it is psychological, relational, and even spiritual.

Importantly, vision-based thinking doesn't require vast wealth to begin. It can start at any income level. Even allocating a small portion of income toward a future-oriented goal—a holiday, training course, investment fund, or donation—can begin to rewire the financial mindset. What matters is not the size of the allocation, but the shift in intentionality. It says, "I am not just surviving. I am directing." This act, repeated over time, becomes the foundation of a new financial identity—one rooted in sovereignty rather than scarcity.

Financial educators and planners increasingly recognise the importance of this paradigm shift. The field of financial therapy, which integrates emotional intelligence with money management, has gained traction for this very reason. As practitioners have observed, no budget will stick, no investment strategy will endure, unless the underlying mindset evolves. Financial expansion is, at its core, a behavioural phenomenon.

The shift from survival to vision also has ripple effects. Individuals who operate from vision mode tend to become multipliers in their communities. They share knowledge, model possibility, mentor others, and create infrastructure—whether through business, philanthropy, or leadership—that uplifts others. In this way, vision becomes not only personal, but collective. It transforms financial growth into a form of civic contribution.

Ultimately, moving from survival to vision is not a destination—it is a discipline. It is a conscious, ongoing practice of resisting fear-based reactivity and cultivating strategy-driven clarity. It is about more than accumulating wealth. It is about expanding what feels possible—financially, emotionally, and existentially.

To live in vision mode is to refuse to be defined by past constraints. It is to see money not only as a means of transaction, but as a medium of transformation. It is to ask not simply, "Can I afford this?" but, "Is this aligned with what I'm building?" In doing so, we reclaim our agency, reframe our narratives, and design financial lives that are not just sustainable—but deeply meaningful.

Embracing Wealth Without Guilt: The Ethics of Thriving Financially

Wealth has always been more than just a matter of numbers. Embedded in its pursuit, possession, and perception are layers of cultural narratives, moral judgments, and personal associations that shape how people feel about money—and about themselves. One of the most pervasive and unspoken barriers to sustained financial growth is guilt: a subtle, often unexamined sense of shame or unworthiness that accompanies the accumulation of wealth. This guilt does not only hinder personal wellbeing; it impairs one's capacity to create impact, steward resources responsibly, and contribute meaningfully to the world.

To understand how to thrive financially without guilt, we must first examine the roots of this discomfort. Guilt around wealth often stems from early moral conditioning. In many families, particularly those with modest means or strong religious affiliations, children grow up with the idea that money is inherently suspect—an object of temptation, greed, or spiritual danger. Phrases such as "money doesn't grow on trees," "filthy rich," or "more money, more problems" are not benign idioms; they are cultural scripts that shape subconscious beliefs. These messages imply that financial success is either the result of exploitation or the precursor to moral compromise.

Such narratives are further reinforced by media depictions. Popular culture has long painted a dichotomy between the "virtuous poor" and the "corrupt rich." Whether in literature, film, or television, wealth is often portrayed as synonymous with arrogance, coldness, or moral bankruptcy, while those who struggle financially are cast as humble, authentic, and deserving. These archetypes can make it profoundly difficult for individuals—especially those committed to social good, creative expression, or ethical entrepreneurship—to feel at ease with their own financial growth. As a result, they may unconsciously self-limit, undercharge, decline opportunities, or dissipate wealth as quickly as it is acquired.

Real-world examples are plentiful. Take the case of Noor, a highly skilled acupuncturist and wellness educator who expanded her practice during the pandemic to meet growing demand. Though her client base flourished and her income increased significantly, she found herself plagued by discomfort. She avoided looking at her bank account, struggled to set sustainable rates, and experienced tension in her relationships when discussing money. On deeper examination, Noor realised she had internalised the belief that her healing work was incompatible with financial abundance—that profit would somehow cheapen her purpose. Through coaching and financial therapy, she began to reframe wealth not as a contradiction to her mission, but as a source of fuel for it. She restructured her business model to include community-access options alongside premium offerings, allowing her to thrive while also honouring her values.

This reframing is crucial. To truly embrace wealth without guilt, one must decouple the concept of money from moral purity or impurity. Money is not inherently good or bad—it is neutral energy. Its ethical dimension arises from its *application* and *intention.* A large income earned through exploitative practices may indeed be ethically questionable. But wealth built through aligned, value-driven work—through service, creativity, innovation, or stewardship—is not only ethical; it is necessary for expanding the reach and resilience of that work. The discomfort around wealth often comes from conflating *means* with *ends*, mistaking the possession of money for the purpose of life. But when money is seen as a tool, not a goal, it becomes a servant of integrity, not a threat to it.

Another layer of wealth guilt arises from comparison. In a world of glaring inequality, it can feel ethically jarring to accumulate wealth while others struggle. This tension is valid—but it should not be paralysing. A healthy response to inequality is not self-imposed austerity, but conscious redistribution and systemic contribution. Those with financial means are uniquely positioned to direct capital towards positive change—through philanthropy, impact investing, fair employment practices, or simply through modelling alternative economic values. Resentment toward wealth often stems from its hoarding, not its existence. When wealth circulates—when it is put in motion with purpose—it benefits not only the individual but the ecosystem around them.

Take for instance the story of Tomas and Lena, co-founders of a sustainable design firm. After landing a major corporate contract, their annual revenue doubled. Instead of shrinking from their new wealth, they leaned into their values. They offered profit-sharing to employees, invested in local community projects, and began mentoring young entrepreneurs from underrepresented backgrounds. Their success did not diminish their ethics; it amplified them. What allowed this was a refusal to be seduced by guilt. They understood that feeling guilty about money was a distraction—that their responsibility lay not in hiding their wealth, but in using it consciously.

From a psychological standpoint, guilt also thrives in silence. Many people carry unspoken discomfort about money because they've never been given language or frameworks to discuss it openly. Money is still a taboo in many households and social circles, particularly in cultures where speaking of wealth is seen as gauche, dangerous, or shameful. This silence breeds ignorance, isolation, and anxiety. One of the most effective antidotes is dialogue—engaging in honest, nuanced conversations about wealth, values, and aspirations. These conversations create space for self-awareness, learning, and ultimately, liberation from inherited scripts.

In practical terms, this shift requires an ongoing commitment to clarity. Individuals who want to thrive financially without guilt must articulate their financial values and align their behaviours accordingly. What does "enough" look like? What role should money play in one's creative, familial, or civic life? What mechanisms—such as giving plans, ethical investments, or community involvement—can ensure that wealth remains rooted in service? These questions do not have one-size-fits-all answers. But asking them consciously reclaims the narrative and transforms guilt into guidance.

Crucially, this work is not only individual. It is cultural. As more people challenge the guilt-wealth binary and model integrated prosperity, new archetypes begin to emerge—archetypes of the generous leader, the resourceful healer, the ethical investor, the thriving activist. These identities disrupt the false dichotomy of spiritual fulfilment versus financial abundance. They suggest a world in which prosperity is not a mark of ego, but of evolution.

Educational institutions, financial advisors, and thought leaders also have a role to play. Financial literacy must move beyond budgeting and investing to include emotional intelligence, identity, and ethics. Wealth coaching and financial therapy are growing fields precisely because they acknowledge that money is never just about math—it is about meaning. As professionals create spaces where clients can explore these dimensions without judgment, they help dismantle the internalised barriers to abundance.

Ultimately, to embrace wealth without guilt is to honour the full expression of human flourishing. It is to say: I do not need to apologise for thriving. I will not shrink my success to soothe the discomfort of others. And I will not confuse sacrifice with virtue when strategy and stewardship can do more good. Guilt may visit us—but it need not reside within us. It is a cue for reflection, not a sentence to stagnation.

By claiming wealth as a natural, deserved, and purposeful dimension of life, individuals liberate not just themselves, but those around them. They become models of what is possible when ethics and abundance meet—not in contradiction, but in collaboration. And in doing so, they rewrite the cultural script: from wealth as shameful to wealth as sovereign, from money as a burden to money as a blessing rightly handled.

The Circle of Expansion: How Mindset, Income, and Opportunity Reinforce Each Other

There exists a subtle yet profound feedback loop that operates beneath the surface of every financial life. It does not begin with a bank balance or a spreadsheet—it begins with mindset. Our beliefs about money shape our behaviours, those behaviours affect our income, and that income expands or contracts the options available to us. These options, in turn, either reinforce our existing mindset or challenge it to grow. This recursive dynamic—what we can call *the circle of expansion*—is one of the most powerful, and often overlooked, forces in personal finance. When this loop is healthy, it can unlock exponential growth. When it is constrained, it can quietly perpetuate stagnation or scarcity.

Understanding this phenomenon requires a departure from the conventional notion that financial success is purely the result of tactical decisions—budgeting, saving, investing. While these tools are indispensable, they operate downstream of belief. As behavioural economists and financial psychologists have increasingly shown, the way individuals *think* about money—what they believe is possible, permissible, or probable—sets the parameters of their financial reality. Change the mindset, and the external metrics eventually follow. Leave it untouched, and even the best strategies will struggle to take root.

Consider the example of Rafael, a first-generation immigrant who was taught from a young age that money is earned through relentless hard work and unflinching frugality. This belief served him well in his early years—he worked multiple jobs, lived below his means, and amassed modest savings. But as he entered his thirties and launched a consultancy, this mindset became limiting. He resisted scaling his business or raising his rates, believing that to do so would be "greedy" or "ungrateful." His income plateaued, his stress increased, and he began to resent his work. Only after engaging in coaching and revisiting these inherited beliefs did he begin to reframe his relationship to money. As his mindset shifted toward sufficiency and self-worth, he began making strategic hires, expanding his client base, and setting fees that reflected his value. His income grew, his time freed up, and his confidence deepened. His new results reinforced his new beliefs, creating a virtuous circle of expansion.

This circular dynamic—mindset to income to opportunity to mindset—is not merely anecdotal. Research in neuroeconomics and positive psychology supports its validity. Studies have shown that individuals who possess what psychologists call a "growth mindset" about finances—believing that their financial capabilities can improve with effort—are more likely to engage in goal-setting, proactive planning, and adaptive risk-taking. These behaviours correlate strongly with upward mobility and financial resilience. Conversely, a "fixed mindset"—marked by beliefs like "I'm just bad with money" or "People like me never get ahead"—correlates with financial avoidance, low savings rates, and under-earning.

The role of income in this feedback loop is equally critical. While mindset sets the trajectory, income provides the fuel. Higher income, when aligned with conscious values, expands the field of available choices: better health care, safer housing, skill-building opportunities, leisure time, and generational support. These choices do not just improve quality of life—they reinforce the belief that financial growth is both possible and sustainable. They create what psychologist Barbara Fredrickson calls a "broaden-and-build" effect, where positive experiences broaden an individual's scope of awareness and build new psychological resources for future success.

Yet the converse is also true. When income is restricted—whether by systemic inequities, self-imposed limits, or unchallenged beliefs—options narrow. People are forced to make decisions from a place of constraint, reinforcing scarcity-based narratives. A mother who turns down a career advancement due to lack of childcare, or an artist who declines a commission out of fear of overcharging, may not be lacking in talent or work ethic—they may simply be caught in a loop where low income reinforces limiting beliefs, which perpetuate low-risk, low-return behaviours.

Breaking out of this loop requires intervention at the belief level. One of the most effective interventions is *evidence-based mindset stretching*. This involves deliberately engaging in behaviours that contradict old narratives, thereby generating new internal data. For example, an individual who believes "No one will pay me more than this" may test that belief by quoting a higher fee to a client—and discovering it is accepted. That singular event can challenge years of internal programming, offering a new narrative: "Maybe I've been underestimating my value."

These belief-disrupting actions are not always comfortable. In fact, they often provoke resistance. But they are essential. Without them, the circle of expansion cannot self-reinforce. It becomes a broken circuit, with mindset disconnected from action and action disconnected from result. When the full loop is intact, each component feeds and strengthens the others. This is the essence of compounding—not just in finance, but in self-perception.

Digital tools can support this process. Budgeting apps that track income growth over time, visual goal-setting platforms, and net worth dashboards all provide tangible proof of progress. This evidence bolsters confidence, which in turn emboldens further action. But technology alone is insufficient without emotional and psychological integration. That is where reflective practices such as journaling, coaching, and peer mentorship come in—providing the space to interrogate old scripts and replace them with new, generative narratives.

One notable case is that of the entrepreneur network Conscious Capital Collective, which focuses on helping business owners integrate wealth consciousness with social impact. Members routinely share not just their revenue growth, but the mindset shifts that enabled it—such as healing money shame, releasing inherited guilt, or embracing ethical ambition. These peer narratives function as collective proof points, expanding what members believe is possible for themselves. In this way, the circle of expansion becomes not just personal, but communal.

Importantly, the circle of expansion must not be mistaken for linear or automatic growth. It is iterative, often messy, and subject to setbacks. Financial dips, rejections, or unproductive habits can temporarily disrupt the loop. But once the core dynamic is understood, recovery becomes quicker. The individual no longer views setbacks as verdicts, but as variables. This psychological flexibility is the hallmark of a healthy feedback loop—it adapts, recalibrates, and continues.

There is also a moral dimension to this model. As individuals expand their capacity to earn, save, and invest, they expand their capacity to influence. Income becomes not just a measure of success, but a multiplier of values. A financially empowered person has more bandwidth to support causes, fund innovations, employ others, and model conscious wealth for their community. In this sense, the circle of expansion is not a selfish pursuit—it is a systemic contribution. When healthy money mindsets circulate within families, organisations, or communities, they create ripple effects that extend far beyond individual bank accounts.

Yet none of this is possible without the foundational realisation: that mindset is not static, income is not destiny, and options are not limited to what one sees today. The circle of expansion begins with a single shift in thought—but it does not end there. It must be reinforced through deliberate behaviour, strategic choices, and continuous reflection. This is not motivational fluff; it is behavioural architecture. It is the difference between a financial life shaped by reaction and one designed through intention.

To live within a healthy circle of expansion is to move from helplessness to agency, from scarcity to sufficiency, from passive endurance to active creation. It is to recognise that money does not change who we are—it reveals the degree to which we believe we are worthy of change. And in this belief lies the quiet, radical power to design a financial life not constrained by fear, but governed by growth.

Risk, Courage, and Financial Growth: Rewiring the Psychology of Bold Decision-Making

Financial growth, particularly the kind that expands not just bank accounts but also personal agency, rarely unfolds in a straight line. It is shaped not merely by strategy but by the psychology of risk-taking—by the willingness to embrace uncertainty, step beyond familiar limits, and act in the presence of fear. Whether it's launching a business, investing in a volatile market, asking for a raise, or pitching a new offer, the capacity to take intelligent risks is a defining feature of financial maturity. Yet for many, risk is synonymous with recklessness. The discomfort it evokes often triggers avoidance, hesitation, or paralysis. To thrive financially, one must cultivate a new relationship with risk—one that is not defined by recklessness, but by courage.

At its core, risk involves making decisions without guaranteed outcomes. It is a confrontation with the unknown. But not all unknowns are created equal. Risk in finance is not a binary variable—it is a continuum. There are measured, strategic risks with asymmetric upside (high potential return, limited downside) and there are blind gambles fuelled by desperation or ego. The distinction lies not in the absence of fear, but in the presence of discernment. This is where psychology becomes paramount: how we perceive, evaluate, and respond to risk determines not only our financial results but our growth trajectory.

Behavioural economics has long studied this phenomenon. Daniel Kahneman and Amos Tversky's pioneering work revealed that humans are far more sensitive to losses than to equivalent gains—a concept known as loss aversion. The fear of losing £100 exerts a stronger emotional impact than the pleasure of gaining the same amount. This bias leads many to avoid opportunities, even when the odds are rationally in their favour. It also explains why individuals may remain in underpaid jobs, avoid investing, or decline to scale a business, despite knowing that stagnation carries its own hidden costs.

To reframe risk, we must reframe fear. Courage is often misunderstood as the absence of fear, when in fact, it is the capacity to act *despite* fear. Neuroscience shows that fear is not just a psychological state—it is a physiological one. When faced with uncertainty, the brain's amygdala activates a threat response, flooding the body with cortisol and adrenaline. This can hijack rational thinking and push individuals toward overly conservative behaviour. However, with awareness and training, individuals can build tolerance for this discomfort and make values-aligned decisions anyway.

One powerful method for doing so is recontextualising risk through narrative. Instead of asking, "What if this goes wrong?", individuals can ask, "What is the cost of *not* doing this?" This reframes risk not as a potential loss, but as a missed opportunity. For example, an entrepreneur who avoids raising prices out of fear of alienating clients might instead ask, "What is the long-term cost of underpricing my value?" Similarly, a professional hesitant to negotiate for higher pay might reflect, "How is staying silent reinforcing systemic undervaluation—not just for me, but for others who come after me?"

Consider the story of Raj, a product manager who had not received a salary increase in four years despite consistently outperforming his targets. He feared that asking for a raise would make him appear ungrateful or risk his position. But after a mentor encouraged him to prepare a value-based pitch, Raj reframed his discomfort. He realised that staying quiet was not neutral—it was complicit in his own undervaluation. He requested a meeting, presented his results and market data, and asked for a 20% raise. His manager agreed without hesitation. Raj's income increased, but more importantly, so did his confidence. That act of courage became a reference point for future negotiations, investments, and leadership decisions. One calculated risk reshaped his self-concept.

This concept of reference points is crucial. Each time an individual takes a smart risk and survives—or better yet, thrives—it reconfigures their mental map. They begin to see themselves as capable of navigating ambiguity. These experiences build what psychologist Albert Bandura termed "self-efficacy"—the belief in one's ability to influence outcomes. High self-efficacy correlates strongly with entrepreneurial success, career advancement, and wealth accumulation.

In business, risk is not optional; it is foundational. No innovation emerges from certainty. Yet many entrepreneurs sabotage their own expansion by avoiding pivotal risks: launching before perfecting, hiring before fully ready, pitching to larger clients, or pivoting in response to market feedback. The difference between those who scale and those who stagnate often lies not in intelligence or funding, but in their risk threshold. Do they have the psychological flexibility to adapt? Can they withstand the ego bruises of failed experiments without abandoning their vision?

Courageous financial growth also involves risk in investing—an arena that triggers deep psychological responses. For first-time investors, the volatility of markets can feel threatening, even immoral. Emotional investing—buying high during euphoria and selling low during panic—is a well-documented pattern. Yet those who cultivate an investor's mindset understand that volatility is not equivalent to loss. They view downturns as buying opportunities and gains as rewards for long-term positioning. They understand the difference between *speculation* and *investment*—and they develop rules for both.

A helpful practice is to evaluate potential risks through the lens of asymmetry. What is the worst-case scenario, and how recoverable is it? What is the best-case scenario, and how transformative might it be? This lens helps to de-escalate fear-based thinking and replace it with strategic calculus. Risk becomes not something to avoid, but something to manage—through diversification, preparation, and reflective decision-making.

Self-advocacy, particularly for marginalised groups, is another frontier where risk and courage intersect. Women, people of colour, and first-generation professionals often navigate unspoken biases when asserting their worth. The act of asking—whether for funding, visibility, or compensation—can feel not just uncomfortable but dangerous. Cultural scripts about humility, deference, or "waiting your turn" compound this anxiety. Yet refusing to ask often ensures structural inequity remains intact.

Supporting this assertion is a growing body of research on the "ask gap"—the phenomenon whereby underrepresented individuals are less likely to negotiate offers or advocate for resources, resulting in cumulative financial disadvantage. Programmes that teach assertiveness, negotiation, and boundary-setting are beginning to close this gap, but the core challenge remains psychological. It is not merely about learning scripts; it is about reclaiming entitlement—not in the pejorative sense, but in the legitimate sense of deserving.

Practical tools help, but mindset shifts do the heaviest lifting. Individuals must begin to see courage not as an act of rebellion, but as a normalised component of financial adulthood. Taking calculated risks is not a betrayal of one's past—it is often a fulfilment of its sacrifices. Risk does not always mean leaving a job, investing in stocks, or launching a startup. It might mean saying "no" to a draining client, testing a new pricing model, or admitting when a strategy is no longer working. These are micro-risks—but they are the building blocks of macro change.

The institutions that shape financial behaviour—schools, families, and workplaces—must also evolve. Risk literacy should be embedded into financial education. Conversations about wealth must include emotional resilience, failure normalisation, and ethical ambition. Only then will individuals develop not just the skill to manage money, but the nerve to pursue meaningful financial growth.

To take risks is to stand at the threshold of possibility. It is to say: I choose not to let fear script my decisions. I am willing to be uncomfortable in pursuit of a more expansive financial life. And I trust that the rewards of acting in integrity—be they material, psychological, or spiritual—are worth the vulnerability it takes to ask, pitch, or invest.

Financial courage is not the absence of risk. It is the art of engaging with risk wisely, creatively, and with full awareness of one's values.

It is a skill that compounds over time, rewriting not only the story of one's finances but the story one tells about who they are and what they're capable of. It is, quite simply, the threshold between where you've been and where you could go—if you dared.

Creating a Financial Environment That Supports You: Designing Systems for Sustainable Wealth

One of the most underestimated variables in long-term financial growth is not talent, discipline, or even knowledge—it is *environment.* Most financial advice focuses on individual behaviour: earn more, save better, invest wisely. But behaviour doesn't happen in a vacuum. It is shaped, nudged, constrained, or reinforced by the environment in which it occurs. Just as elite athletes design training spaces that optimise performance, those who wish to build sustainable wealth must design financial environments that support, rather than sabotage, their ambitions. This is not a matter of aesthetics or convenience; it is a matter of structure, psychology, and alignment.

To create an environment that supports financial expansion, we must consider five key arenas: physical space, digital systems, time architecture, social relationships, and internal narratives. Each of these functions as either a lever or a limiter. When thoughtfully calibrated, they reduce friction, increase clarity, and make success feel less like a grind and more like a flow.

The physical workspace, though seemingly trivial, exerts a subtle but powerful influence on financial behaviour. A cluttered desk often mirrors a cluttered mental state, where bills go unpaid, receipts are lost, and administrative tasks get deferred. In contrast, a clean, intentional workspace invites focus, proactivity, and respect for the tasks at hand. Research from the Princeton Neuroscience Institute has shown that physical clutter competes for our attention, reducing performance and increasing stress. For entrepreneurs, freelancers, and remote workers, the difference between financial stagnation and momentum may lie, in part, in whether their environment cues discipline or distraction.

Digital tools serve as the nervous system of a modern financial life. Automated transfers, budgeting apps, visual dashboards, tax preparation software—these are not luxuries; they are scaffolding. Their true power lies not merely in functionality but in automation. When systems are automated, decision fatigue decreases, and consistency improves. For instance, setting up an automatic monthly transfer into a high-interest savings account eliminates the need to negotiate with oneself about saving. It enforces a behaviour that, left to willpower alone, might occur sporadically or not at all. The best financial environments do not rely on constant motivation—they are designed to make default actions the right ones.

Time, too, is a form of capital. Yet it is often squandered on low-leverage tasks that offer little financial return. A supportive environment includes a *calendar architecture* that prioritises revenue-generating activity and strategic thinking. For example, blocking out weekly time for financial review—analysing income streams, forecasting expenses, updating goals—transforms money management from an occasional crisis response to a normalised routine. Those who integrate financial stewardship into their regular rhythms report lower anxiety, increased confidence, and more strategic decision-making. They stop reacting to money and start *directing* it.

The social environment is perhaps the most powerful—and the most overlooked—dimension of financial growth. As social creatures, humans are deeply influenced by the attitudes, norms, and behaviours of those around them. If you are surrounded by people who see wealth as corrupt, risky, or out of reach, it becomes difficult to embody a different narrative without guilt or friction. Conversely, proximity to financially empowered peers normalises success, expands perspective, and offers practical knowledge that cannot be gleaned from books alone.

Consider the example of Tanya, a graphic designer who had long kept her rates low due to fear of client rejection. After joining a mastermind group of creative entrepreneurs, she discovered her pricing was not only under-market but unsustainable. The group's encouragement and transparency gave her the confidence to raise her rates by 40%. Not only did she retain most clients, but she also attracted new ones who respected her pricing and professionalism. The shift wasn't due to a new skill—it was due to a new *context.*

The environments we participate in online matter, too. Social media can reinforce scarcity thinking or inflate consumerist urges depending on the algorithms we feed. Curating one's digital inputs—following financially literate voices, engaging in investor forums, subscribing to high-quality newsletters—creates a daily immersion in content that informs and inspires rather than distracts and distorts. These are not trivial decisions. They shape what we believe is possible and influence the actions we are willing to take.

Equally important is the emotional and psychological environment—the internal space in which financial decisions are made. No budgeting app can compensate for an inner critic that says, "You're bad with money." No investment plan can thrive in the shadow of guilt, shame, or impostor syndrome. A supportive financial environment includes regular introspective practices that help surface, question, and reframe limiting beliefs. Journaling, coaching, therapy, and even somatic practices like breathwork or meditation are not ancillary—they are essential. They help ensure that your internal environment doesn't sabotage your external efforts.

This inner work often leads to re-anchoring one's financial identity. Instead of seeing oneself as someone who "just scrapes by" or "isn't good with numbers," the narrative becomes one of conscious stewardship, strategic growth, and self-trust. This shift ripples outward. A new identity influences new habits, which reinforce new outcomes, which further strengthen the identity. It is a loop—but it begins with context.

Creating a supportive financial environment is not a one-time event—it is an iterative process. Life stages shift, goals evolve, relationships change, and systems must adapt. The key is intentional design: asking, at regular intervals, *Does my current environment reflect and support the wealth I intend to build?* If not, what tweaks—small or large—can make alignment easier, and resistance less frequent?

Financial environments are not about luxury or optimisation for its own sake. They are about integrity—about aligning the structure of daily life with one's financial values and vision. When your environment is in sync with your aspirations, wealth-building ceases to be a constant uphill climb. It becomes a well-supported ascent.

This isn't theory—it is architectural psychology applied to the realm of money. It respects the reality that willpower is finite, that human beings are cue-responsive creatures, and that success is rarely the product of heroism but often the result of smart design. When you make the right behaviours easier and the wrong ones harder, you don't need more discipline—you need less.

Ultimately, wealth is not built in spreadsheets alone. It is built in the quiet choices of everyday design: the apps you trust, the people you call, the messages you consume, the spaces you inhabit, and the beliefs you carry. If these are coherent with your financial aspirations, they will lift you forward with a subtle but relentless grace. If they are not, you will find yourself fighting invisible currents.

Design wisely. The environment you choose—or fail to choose—will shape not just your bank account, but your belief in what you're truly capable of creating.

Conclusion
The Reset is Just the Beginning

You were never truly "bad with money." What you inherited, more often than not, was a script—quiet, unspoken, and rarely examined—that has been passed down through generations and silently replayed in your financial habits. Perhaps it was shaped by parents who lived in fear of instability, or by cultural expectations that equate modesty with virtue, or even by an education system that never bothered to teach the basics—let alone the nuanced emotions tied to earning, spending, or saving. The truth is, most people aren't broken financially; they're simply running on outdated programming.

This book has never aimed to hand you quick fixes or clever budgeting tricks. Instead, it's been a call to recalibrate how you see money—not as a puzzle of numbers to be cracked, but as a deeply human experience to be understood, navigated, and ultimately empowered. We've moved beyond balance sheets and spreadsheets to explore the scripts beneath—the beliefs, emotional patterns, generational wounds, language, habits, and environments that shape your financial life. And out of that exploration, a more profound truth emerges: financial transformation isn't a finish line. It's a lens.

When you change the way you perceive money, you start to shift your relationship with yourself. No longer is your value tied to your paycheck or your past missteps. You begin to recognise the emotional signals that spark impulsive spending, chronic under-earning, or fear-fuelled hoarding. More importantly, you learn to intervene—gently but deliberately—when those old patterns try to regain control. And above all, you start making choices based on alignment with your values and vision, rather than out of fear or social conformity.

This is what it means to live a reset life: to consciously step away from someone else's programming and replace it with a system that reflects your own, ever-evolving priorities. Not a flawless system—there's no such thing—but one that's flexible, self-aware, and responsive to the complexities you face day to day.

Take Elena, for instance, a schoolteacher who once labelled herself financially illiterate. For years, she avoided her bank statements, left important decisions to others, and masked her discomfort behind a facade of stoicism. But as she worked through the principles shared here, she began to journal her money beliefs, uncovering a deep-rooted sense of unworthiness inherited from a household where women simply didn't talk about finances. Slowly, she took brave steps: automating savings, renegotiating her salary, investing in her professional growth. Her change wasn't dramatic or cinematic, but it was profound. For the first time, her financial decisions were guided not by guilt or shame, but by clarity.

What Elena—and countless others—discover is that financial growth is never really "done." Hitting a milestone isn't the finish line; it's the start of a new baseline. True wealth—measured not just in currency, but in autonomy, peace of mind, and freedom of choice—demands ongoing attention. Like physical fitness or emotional intelligence, it's a lifelong relationship requiring regular check-ins, adjustments, and recommitment.

Practically, this means returning to your beliefs often. Asking yourself, "Does this thought still serve the life I want to create?" It means seeing your budget not as a rigid exercise in sacrifice, but as a living expression of your values. It means re-examining your financial environment, pruning what no longer fits, and nurturing what supports your growth. And it means granting yourself grace to err without spiralling into self-reproach.

There will be times when old programming creeps back—when a trigger unleashes a scarcity spiral or social media sparks comparison. This is not failure; it's maintenance. And while maintenance rarely feels as thrilling as breakthrough, it is where true mastery takes shape.

So the reset isn't a destination. It's a doorway. The beginning of a new financial agency—one founded not on rigid control or reckless abandon, but on discernment, resilience, and self-trust.

There's a quiet power in that. Once you trust yourself with money—not just as an abstract concept, but as a lived, embodied reality—you stop chasing certainty. You cease seeking others' validation for your financial choices. You no longer outsource your authority. And in this space, fresh possibilities begin to bloom. Possibilities for wealth that feels as good as it looks. For generosity that isn't a show, but deeply purposeful. For ambition that honours your nervous system as much as your net worth.

Financial freedom, reframed this way, isn't about dodging responsibility or chasing some mythical state of passive income nirvana. It's about having the capacity to respond—to challenges, to opportunities, to your shifting purpose—with integrity and confidence. It's about becoming the author of your financial life, rather than a mere executor of someone else's script.

As you move forward, don't ask, "Am I finished?" Instead, ask, "What am I building now?" Because, in truth, every decision—every purchase, every investment, every conversation about money—is a brick in the architecture of your future. And the blueprint matters far less than the awareness you bring to the building process.

You have reset not just your mindset, but your very lens. Now, the task is to live through it—to let it shape not only your bank statements but your self-worth, your relationships, your choices, and ultimately, your legacy.

If that sounds daunting, well, it is. But it's also some of the most meaningful, liberating, and profoundly human work you'll ever do.

This is no ending. It's the first draft of a new beginning—one you get to revise, refine, and reimagine on your own terms, in your own time. Keep at it. The true wealth lies not just in the destination, but in the awareness that, at last, you are the one holding the pen.

You're Not "Bad with Money"—You've Been Running Someone Else's Program

For most people who struggle with money, the issue isn't intelligence, laziness, or even discipline. It is programming. Deep, often invisible frameworks of thought, emotion, and expectation that were adopted long before the first paycheque arrived. We absorb these frameworks from parents, culture, religion, media, school systems, and social circles. And then, without ever giving explicit permission, we begin to live by them. These borrowed scripts—some outdated, others outright harmful—become the operating systems that silently dictate how we think about earning, spending, saving, and deserving.

To be "bad with money" is a story, not a diagnosis. And like all stories, it can be rewritten. But to rewrite it, we must first understand its origin.

Childhood offers the earliest exposure to financial behaviour, but not always through explicit lessons. For many, it was what wasn't said that carried the most weight. Silence around money often communicates shame. Witnessing arguments about bills, feeling the tension of financial insecurity, or observing a parent self-sacrifice to the point of depletion—these experiences encode beliefs more powerfully than any lecture. They tell the child, *Money is a source of stress. It's better not to talk about it. People fight over it. We don't have enough. And we probably never will.*

As adults, these beliefs manifest in myriad ways: undercharging for services, overspending to feel momentary control or validation, avoiding investment decisions, or feeling guilt when things go well. A person may intellectually understand that budgeting is smart or that investing early is wise, but still find themselves unable to act on that knowledge. That isn't ignorance—it's conflict between conscious logic and unconscious programming.

Real-world case studies abound. Consider Leah, a freelance consultant in her mid-30s who consistently underpriced her work despite glowing testimonials and repeat clients. After some exploration, she realised she had internalised the belief that "helping people shouldn't come at a cost." This belief stemmed from watching her mother—a social worker—struggle financially despite being admired for her generosity. Leah's pricing, it turned out, wasn't based on market research but on a loyalty to an identity that equated service with self-sacrifice. Once she recognised this, she was able to separate the value she delivered from the guilt she had learned to feel when receiving. Her pricing structure shifted, and so did her client relationships—marked now by clearer boundaries and mutual respect.

These scripts run deep. And they are not always wrong in content, but they are often wrong in context. What served your family in the past—perhaps thrift in times of war, or distrust of banks following economic collapse—may not serve your goals in the present. Yet without interrogation, inherited beliefs continue operating beneath awareness. You might be living by principles that no longer apply to your economy, your values, or your vision.

This is why financial transformation is not simply about changing numbers; it's about changing the narratives behind them. And that change, to be sustainable, must be relational. It must include not only what you believe about money, but what you believe about yourself. Many financial struggles are secondary symptoms of distorted self-perception: I'm not good enough. I don't deserve ease. If I succeed, I'll be judged. These are not money problems—they are identity distortions playing out through financial decisions.

To recalibrate, start by asking different questions. Instead of "Why can't I stick to a budget?" ask "What story am I living that makes budgeting feel like punishment?" Instead of "Why do I never have enough?" ask "Whose voice is telling me what 'enough' looks like?" This shift in inquiry turns shame into insight and confusion into clarity. It moves you from helplessness to authorship.

This reset is not about perfection. It is about perspective. A person who has grown up in survival mode cannot be expected to seamlessly adopt behaviours associated with long-term wealth planning. Trusting in abundance, delaying gratification, taking strategic risks—these all require psychological safety. That safety isn't built overnight. It is built through repeated, intentional acts of self-trust. Paying a bill on time. Asking for what you're worth. Saying no to obligations that deplete you. Automating your savings. These are small actions, but they are massive reprogramming events. Each one sends a new signal to your nervous system: *We are safe. We are capable. We are building.*

This is where recalibration becomes essential. Even as your external circumstances shift, your internal framework must catch up. Someone who earns more than they ever have before might still feel poor. Someone who has paid off debt may still feel like they're one mistake away from ruin. The subconscious takes time to adjust. Without regular reflection and recalibration, old beliefs can resurface, distorting perception and sabotaging progress.

This is why financial transformation must be seen as a lifelong lens—not a single pivot point. A lens means you never stop seeing through it. You view decisions, relationships, opportunities, and setbacks all through a recalibrated framework. And that framework grows with you. It evolves as you do.

For example, early in your financial healing, success might mean finally sticking to a budget. Later, it might mean giving generously without fear. Later still, it could mean walking away from a lucrative but misaligned opportunity without guilt. Each of these acts requires a different layer of self-knowledge and trust. The core of the transformation is not what you do with money—but who you become in relation to it.

What does this look like in daily life? It means developing an ongoing relationship with your finances that includes regular check-ins—not just for budgeting, but for belief auditing. Are you acting from old fear or new vision? Are your goals reactive or proactive? Are you chasing security, or are you designing fulfilment?

It also means surrounding yourself with environments that reinforce your new mindset. Community, mentorship, digital content, and professional support all shape the financial ecosystem in which you operate. You cannot heal a scarcity mindset while being immersed in narratives of fear and comparison. Your environment must reflect and support your intentions, or you'll find yourself defaulting to old patterns not out of weakness, but out of habit.

None of this is about blame. It is about responsibility—the powerful, liberating kind that says: *I may not have chosen the original program, but I can choose to rewrite it.* That rewriting does not have to be dramatic. In fact, the most lasting changes often begin quietly: choosing different words, practising gratitude for what is working, making decisions one level above where fear wants to keep you.

The reset, then, is not an endpoint. It's a new operating system. One that honours where you've been but does not make you a prisoner of it. One that welcomes evolution, tolerates imperfection, and celebrates growth that is measured not only in income, but in self-trust, clarity, and courage.

You are not "bad with money." You are a person who has inherited beliefs, adapted to systems, and responded to pressures—often without conscious choice. Now, with awareness, you are reclaiming that choice. That's not a small thing. That's everything.

Let this not be the closing of your financial story, but the reinvigoration of your authorship. Let it be a reminder that your wealth begins not in your wallet, but in your worldview. And that every recalibration—no matter how small—is an act of sovereignty.

The reset is just the beginning. Now you begin again—smarter, braver, and finally, on your terms.

About the Author

Rami de Vries is a wealth strategist and mindset coach with a multicultural background and a passion for unlocking human potential. Blending behavioural finance, neuroscience, and ancient philosophy, he helps individuals reprogram their limiting beliefs around money and success. Having worked with clients across Europe, the Middle East, and North America, Rami offers a global perspective on what it means to cultivate abundance—not just in income, but in thought. The Wealth Mindset Reset is his blueprint for those ready to shift from scarcity to limitless possibility.

www.ingramcontent.com/pod-product-compliance
Lightning Source LLC
Chambersburg PA
CBHW031346230926
51848CB00002B/401
* 9 7 8 9 3 7 1 3 4 3 2 5 1 *

groups, community workshops, or peer networks—can reduce shame and normalise the emotional dimensions of finance. Hearing others articulate their struggles often helps individuals contextualise their own, transforming a solitary burden into a shared human experience. It is in this space of collective acknowledgement that new narratives and strategies can emerge.

Importantly, money healing is not about bypassing practical action. It is about sequencing it correctly. Rather than starting with budgeting or investing, individuals affected by financial trauma may need to begin with regulation—cultivating emotional and physiological stability in the presence of financial stressors. From that base, they can begin to make choices that are not reactive but intentional. Healing creates the internal conditions necessary for sustainable financial growth.

This healing process is also inherently non-linear. Just as trauma is cumulative, healing unfolds in layers. Progress may be followed by setbacks, confidence may give way to doubt, and success may surface unexpected emotions. This does not signal failure. It is part of the recalibration of the nervous system and identity. With patience and support, new patterns take hold—not through force, but through repetition, safety, and conscious engagement.

At a cultural level, recognising financial trauma invites a more compassionate and effective model of financial literacy. It challenges the myth that people who struggle with money simply lack discipline or intelligence. It repositions financial wellbeing not as a purely technical skill but as an integrative process involving mental health, emotional intelligence, social context, and self-awareness. This paradigm shift does not dilute financial responsibility—it enriches it. When people feel seen and supported in their full humanity, they are more likely to engage with their finances, take ownership of their choices, and build resilience over time.

Ultimately, addressing the role of financial trauma is not only a psychological necessity; it is an ethical one. If we want to create systems and societies that promote true financial inclusion, we must start by acknowledging the invisible wounds that distort financial agency. By integrating money healing into personal finance